Plough Quarterly

BREAKING GROUND FOR A RENEWED W

Winter 2015, Number 3

Artists: Pablo Picasso, Carlton Murrell, Pierre-Auguste Renoir, John Singer Sargent, Konstantin Makovsky, Victor Borisov Musatov, John Everett Millais, Philipp Otto Runge

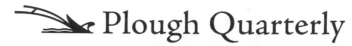

Plough Quarterly

BREAKING GROUND FOR A RENEWED WORLD

www.plough.com

Plough Quarterly features original stories, ideas, and culture to inspire everyday faith and action. Starting from the conviction that the teachings and example of Jesus can transform and renew our world, we aim to apply them to all aspects of life, seeking common ground with all people of goodwill regardless of creed. The goal of *Plough Quarterly* is to build a living network of readers, contributors, and practitioners so that, in the words of Hebrews, we may "spur one another on toward love and good deeds."

Plough Quarterly is published by Plough, the publishing house of the Bruderhof, an international movement of Christian communities whose members are called to follow Jesus together in the spirit of the Sermon on the Mount and of the first church in Jerusalem, sharing all talents, income, and possessions (Acts 2 and 4). Bruderhof communities, which include both families and single people from a wide range of backgrounds, are located in the United States, England, Germany, Australia, and Paraguay. Visitors are welcome at any time. To learn more about the Bruderhof's faith, history, and daily life, or to find a community near you to arrange a visit, go to *www.bruderhof.com.*

Editors: Peter Mommsen, Sam Hine, Maureen Swinger. Art director: Emily Alexander.
Web editor: Carole Vanderhoof. Contributing editors: Veery Huleatt, Charles Moore, Chungyon Won.

Founding Editor: Eberhard Arnold (1883–1935)

Plough Quarterly No. 3: Childhood
Published by Plough Publishing House, ISBN 978-0-87486-608-7
Copyright © 2014 by Plough Publishing House. All rights reserved.

Editorial Office
PO Box 398
Walden, NY 12586
T: 845.572.3455
info@plough.com

Subscriber Services
PO Box 345
Congers, NY 10920-0345
T: 800.521.8011
subscriptions@plough.com

United Kingdom
Brightling Road
Robertsbridge
TN32 5DR
T: +44(0)1580.883.344

Australia
4188 Gwydir Highway
Elsmore, NSW
2360 Australia
T: +61(0)2.6723.2213

Plough Quarterly (ISSN 2372-2584) is published quarterly by Plough Publishing House, PO Box 398, Walden, NY 12586.
Individual subscription $32 per year in the United States; Canada add $8, other countries add $16.
Application to mail at periodicals postage pricing is pending at Walden, NY and additional mailing offices.
POSTMASTER: Send address changes to *Plough Quarterly,* PO Box 345, Congers, NY 10920-0345.

Fritz Eichenberg, detail, *The Peaceable Kingdom*

Dear Reader,

"A little child shall lead them," writes the prophet Isaiah, imagining a coming age when "the wolf shall live with the lamb, the leopard shall lie down with the kid, the calf and the lion and the fatling together."

Amidst the surfeit of books, programs, and online resources on parenting and education, it's easy to conclude that there's nothing new to say about childhood. And at least to those who aren't parents or educators, the whole topic may seem over-hyped.

But childhood and children matter immensely – especially to followers of the one who taught his hearers that they must "change and become like children" in order to share in the future age that Isaiah foretold (Matt. 18:3).

The idea of childhood innocence, certain social historians and evolutionary biologists tell us, is a modern invention, a mere sentimental fantasy. But while the experience of childhood has undeniably changed over the centuries, Jesus' words remind us of truths that remain unchanged. The mystery of being a child, and of becoming a child, is central to the gospel, and has been so from the start.

This issue opens with "Discovering Reverence" by Johann Christoph Arnold, whose new book *Their Name Is Today: Reclaiming Childhood in a Hostile World* (just released by Plough!) raises a host of urgent questions. In response, a surgeon shares what he's learned from children with disabilities. Dispatches from Ferguson, Missouri, the US–Mexico border, the South Bronx, and America's kindergartens focus on places where childhood is especially threatened. Other contributors examine public, homeschool, and Christian education; highlight the role that fathers play; and grapple with Jesus' uncomfortable version of family values.

The escalating violence in Iraq and Syria is another heartrending reminder that Isaiah's vision of the peaceable kingdom has yet to be realized. These horrors also pose a tough challenge to those who are committed to Jesus' way of nonviolent love: Is it still possible to insist on the absolute nonviolence taught by the early Christians and Martin Luther King Jr.? We ask this question of Ron Sider, a leading pacifist, in an interview on page 56.

Do you have reactions, stories, or insights to share? How can we better put the gospel into practice? We look forward to hearing from you. In the words from Hebrews, let's keep "spurring one another on to faith and good deeds."

Warm greetings,

Peter

Peter Mommsen
Editor

The Joy of Confession

First of all I wish to express my wholehearted agreement with Steve Clifford's "Purity in a Porn Age" [Summer 2014]. Porn coupled with the computer is surely one of the disasters of our age. What adds to that danger is that little ones can see it without their parents' control. Porn indeed reduces the human being to a Thing. And then there is the tragedy of addiction.

Steve's "four steps" reflect Catholic teaching, particularly the last step, which for us Catholics is the Sacrament of Confession (or "Reconciliation" as it is named after Vatican II). Even from a purely human point of view, "a joy shared is a joy doubled; a burden shared is a burden halved." In fact, through the priest confessor we share this burden directly with Jesus. And we take courage in the words of Jesus, "There will be greater joy in heaven at the conversion of one sinner than over a hundred just men."

Frank Mascarenhas

Pacifists in Alcatraz

On Duane Stoltzfus's "The Martyrs of Alcatraz," Summer 2014: I left the Marine Corps as a conscientious objector after fifteen years, and joined the Mennonite Church in October 2001. Even today being a conscientious objector is difficult. I am ridiculed by many Christians because I will no longer fight and kill for an earthly empire.

Micheal J. McEvoy

Bonhoeffer among the Assassins

This debate, like most debates on Christian pacifism, misses the point [Charles Moore, "Was Bonhoeffer Willing to Kill?", Summer 2014]. The biblical Christ did not teach "pacifism" or resistance to evil by nonviolent means. If you want to follow Christ, then "love your enemies." That's the cost of discipleship. I wouldn't look to Bonhoeffer for an example though. Nor the rest of us.

Christopher Russell

Katharina Hutter, Tyrolean Martyr

On Jason Landsel's "Katharina Hutter, Heroine of the Radical Reformation," Summer 2014: We are counseled in God's Word to buy from him "gold refined by fire" (Revelation 3:18). Katharina and Jakob understood the eternal value of the Gospel of the kingdom of God. Their sacrifice for the living of a life of genuine faith showed forth the full value of being willing to give up everything, in order to gain everything. May such an example reach through the ages and warm our hearts and spirits to live life today with similar dedication to our God.

Randy Hall

What Kind of Church Did Jesus Want?

Kwon Jeong-saeng's words are beautiful and true ["The Church I Dreamed Of," Autumn 2014]. How often do we look elsewhere for God's kingdom rather than right in front of our eyes! In the Lord's Prayer we pray: "Thy kingdom come, thy will be done, on earth as it is in heaven." Do we believe that in heaven some people will be living in mansions while others will be living in garbage dumps? Do we believe that a few will be feasting while others are starving? Do we believe that in the kingdom it will be God's will to destroy the lands and pollute the waters? Do we believe that in heaven there will be walls and borders to separate people? If we do not believe that it is God's will in heaven, why do think it is acceptable here on God's earth?

Patrick Carolan

Real Heroes

This "post-heroic age" logic has been applied within Christianity, too [Maximilian Probst, "Heroes: Now It's Your Turn," Autumn 2014]. I can't tell you how many times I've heard the words, "But Jesus doesn't mean we're *all* supposed to do this," or "By 'sell all you have and give to the poor,' he meant to not make an idol out of money." It's as if giving your life completely to Jesus is an outdated and extreme response. We do still need heroes, like Mother Teresa and Saint Patrick; I just wish Christians wouldn't preach as though the heroic characteristics of such people were no longer achievable, or even desirable!

Ryan Albosta

We welcome letters to the editor. Letters and web comments may be edited for length and clarity, and may be published in any medium. Letters should be sent with the writer's name and address to letters@plough.com.

Spreading Love and Fidelity on Campus

Pop culture and even professors are telling college students that personal happiness is the greatest good, that anything goes, and that marriage is outdated. Is anyone telling them the truth: that true fulfillment is found through living lives of sexual integrity and in the commitment of lifelong marriage? That is the core mission of the Love and Fidelity Network. Founded in response to the one-sided conversation about matters concerning marriage, family, and sexuality at Princeton University in 2007, LFN now has a presence on more than two dozen college campuses.

Rooted in the belief that "the flourishing of society depends on healthy family lives and stable marriages," the network includes students, graduates, instructors, and others committed to sexual integrity and the importance of marriage and family life. Through poster campaigns, student organizations, speaker events, and national conferences, they equip students to encourage their peers to embrace "a healthier and more responsible way of living out their sexuality, and prepare for their own future marriages and families."

www.loveandfidelity.org

Working with the Humility of Mary

For decades, the Humility of Mary Volunteer Service has been faithfully deploying volunteers to areas of need. Catholic sisters work alongside young people as they grow into their place of service in inner-city neighborhoods and migrant communities. Volunteers live simply and communally, sharing with their coworkers, fellow volunteers, and the nuns in the field or at Villa Maria, the community center in Pulaski, Pennsylvania. Stepping out of college for a few weeks, a year, or longer, volunteers find themselves immersed in work more challenging and fulfilling than any academic course: community outreach, women's issues, farming, literacy projects, refugee support, and legal aid, to name a few.

Aside from practical guidance and counsel, anyone who signs up for this program can count on another benefit. They will join a growing list of names which the elderly nuns at Villa Maria peruse daily, so as to be specific in their intercessory prayers, a task they've taken on after years of active service.

www.humilityofmary.org

Babies against Bullying

When Mary Gordon of Toronto founded Roots of Empathy in 1996, she had a far-reaching goal: "to build caring, peaceful, and civil societies through the development of empathy in children and adults." But she observed that her best anti-bullying teacher did not have a degree in sociology. How could he? He was only three months old.

In the Roots of Empathy program, a parent and baby from the community visit a classroom nine times over the course of a school year. A program instructor accompanies the family to guide children as they observe the loving relationship between baby and parent, and note how the baby is growing and changing over the course of the year.

Children learn to understand the baby's perspective and feelings, and can extend their learning toward a better understanding of their own feelings and those of others. This emotional literacy lays the foundation for more safe and caring classrooms. Children who are socially and emotionally competent are much more likely to challenge cruelty and injustice, and stand up for the defenseless. Teachers and instructors have documented amazing long-term changes in children's behavior. As the prophet Isaiah wrote over 2500 years ago, "A little child shall lead them."

www.rootsofempathy.org

Photograph by Susie Huleatt

Sending Messages into the Future

ELSE ARNOLD

Above, the village of Keilhau, Germany, in Friedrich Fröbel's "valley of education"

"Children are the living messages we send to a time we will not see."

Neil Postman

A recent visitor to the tiny Thuringian village of Keilhau, home to eighty-six inhabitants and the last stop on Germany's longest cul-de-sac, called it "the end of the world." But we who work here know that Keilhau is a place where broken worlds are healed, a place which sends new messages out into the future every year. It was here that Friedrich Fröbel, the groundbreaking nineteenth-century educator and inventor of the kindergarten, founded his first school and wrote his magnum opus *The Education of Man.* His premise: "Education should lead and guide the human being to inward clarity, to peace with nature, and to unity with God."

In 1817, Fröbel first looked down on Keilhau from a nearby mountain and exclaimed, "What a valley for education!" Weeks later he moved into an abandoned barn with his first five students. Between lessons, they built their first school building and explored the local mountains. Outside the original house is a plaque with Fröbel's words inscribed: "I want to educate independent thinkers and people who take initiative."

Nearly two hundred years later, Keilhau is still a haven where children find peace and independence. But while Fröbel took in the sons of the well-to-do, Keilhau now receives disadvantaged children with learning disabilities, many from troubled homes. M, for example, recently arrived from a psychiatric unit. He usually spends recess huddled against a wall, panic in his eyes at the chaos of footballs, hula hoops, and scooters racing around him. But yesterday I found him squatting on the playground, oblivious of the other children. I was struck by the transformation. "Look," he whispered in response to my greeting. "I have to protect this moth – it has a broken leg."

How can we help the most vulnerable and hurt children? In his book, Fröbel answers: "Play is the purest, most spiritual activity of man. . . . It gives joy, freedom, contentment, inner and outer rest, and peace with the world." I often watch the children playing out their fears, but I also see them find peace through play.

J is a second grader from a fragmented home; "Papa" is any one of about fifteen men who come in and out of his life. Recently, we took the children into the woods for the afternoon, to explore, build huts, and discover insects. While the other children played around him, J sat in a "hut" of old branches, quietly counting and arranging pinecones. The area around him filled with an almost holy peace as he made order of his life.

Fröbel's maxim, "Education is example and love," has spread all over the world from this tiny valley. It has shaped the Bruderhof's education for the last eighty years, since Annemarie Wächter, a Fröbel family descendent, left her childhood home in Keilhau to join the community in 1932. She brought Fröbel's legacy with her, sharing it with the other members and with her own children, including Johann Christoph Arnold [see page 10].

And so, from Keilhau and from other schools like it all over the world, messengers are sent out into the future ready to work with their hands, to delight in nature, and to demonstrate that small acts of love can change lives. ✈

Else Arnold, a member of the Bruderhof communities, has taught at the Freie Fröbelschule Keilhau since 2007, as part of a collaboration to apply the ideas of Fröbel to the care and education of at-risk children.

Seizing Moments of Awe

BILL WISER

Photograph by Roger Groom, *astrophotography.com.au*

Another Australian evening is coming on. Soon the setting sun will burnish the contrasting orange and silver patterns of a gum tree's bark and deepen the glowing pink of the galahs' feathers as the birds find their roost for the night.

It is time to be enveloped once again by a vast silence interrupted only occasionally by the irreverent laughter of a kookaburra or the raucous screech of a homing sulphur-crested cockatoo.

When the sun sets in the northern tablelands of New South Wales, the near-vertical ecliptic can create a sudden plunge from daylight into darkness. And on clear winter nights the swath of the Milky Way extends from the Swan in the north to the luminous star clouds and dark dust lanes extending from the Archer to the Southern Cross. Viewed in one piece, the effect is breathtaking.

The Southern Cross is lovely and deserves its iconic position on the flags of five nations. But it is the Scorpion that commands center stage within the Milky Way – tail coiled for the painful strike, pincers outstretched ready to capture the unsuspecting wanderer.

Lately a mythic drama played out overhead as the planet Mars was inexorably drawn into the claws of the constellation. It passed within three degrees of Antares, a reddish star imbedded in the Scorpion, whose name means "the rival of Mars," having about the same brightness and color as the planet. The ancients who named this red giant did not know that Antares far exceeds the size of our sun; in fact, were it to sit in the center of our solar system, its outer rim would extend beyond the orbit of Mars.

Silence, solitude, sunset, and stars have a softening effect on the human spirit. Under their influence, our mundane concerns – what poet Philip Britts called the "day-long tap of thoughts" and the "trivial tinkle of the day" – are gradually replaced by wonder. As Rabbi Abraham Joshua Heschel notes, this sense of wonder is not simply of passing worth; rather, it forms the very root of faith itself and nurtures a wisdom that no amount of knowledge can replicate:

> Wisdom comes from awe rather than from shrewdness. It is evoked not in moments of calculation but in moments of being in rapport with the mystery of reality. The greatest insights happen to us in moments of awe.

We would do well, then, not to miss such opportunities as come our way – and they will do so no matter the setting, if our hearts are attuned to them.

Bill Wiser lives in Elsmore, New South Wales, Australia.

The Southern Cross, seen through trees

Daring to Sing

Those aren't the words I know. My son is sprawled on the rug, hitching up a tractor and trailer, and taking liberties with lyrics. There aren't enough machines mentioned in his song repertoire, so he's re-purposing "This Land Is Your Land." Woodie Guthrie's song is being populated with excavators and front-end loaders. Not that Guthrie would object – his songs often grew new verses or underwent spontaneous substitutions.

I believe that music is every child's birthright. I'm not talking about canned music, shrilling through speakers or ear buds, synthesized and sterile. I mean songs with humble origins, growing, changing, shared among friends on a winter evening – songs that celebrate the seasons of the planet and the heart.

The professionalism of commercial music may have scared us away from attempting our own unpolished melodies. If so, we need to climb back into childhood and lose our self-consciousness along the way. Perhaps the best time to do that is at Christmas, when in public places we're bombarded with every tune from the sacred to the inane.

Last year, I was toting my son along in my shopping cart, dodging through the Christmas crush, when he looked up into my face in alarm. "Why did they just do that?"

"What?" I whipped around, looking for an altercation.

"No," he said. "In the music. They just ran 'Jingle Bells' into 'Away in a Manger.'" I hadn't heard anything more than seamless background noise. He had heard a collision of two unrelated songs.

Does he have an aversion to 'Jingle Bells'? No. We live in the country; he's ridden in a sleigh; it jingled, jolly good fun in January. Does it relate to a baby who had no crib for a bed? Not really. Children are hungry for meaning, for a song they can claim as their own. Our favorite Christmas song is a simple dedication to the baby without a crib:

Advent, we are waiting for Advent
   with your candles,
for now in this darkness
   the light will come once more.

This year a new verse appeared: "Jesus, we are waiting for Jesus, with your kingdom." A child's longing for a special birth now reaches toward rebirth for all people. ➤

Maureen Swinger

2. Advent, we are waiting for Advent, with your angels....

3. Christmas, we are waiting for Christmas, with your manger....

William Merritt Chase, detail, *Topaz Grapes*

From WikiArt (public domain)

Setting the Table at Koinonia Farm

BREN DUBAY

Tending the garden was humankind's first task. In the words of Genesis 2:15: "The Lord God then took the man and settled him in the garden of Eden, to cultivate and care for it." Today, however, there is growing alarm that the way we have been cultivating is bringing our planet to the brink of destruction.

Following World War II, modern agriculture set out to feed the world. In order to produce more food, we adopted the use of synthetic herbicides, pesticides, and fungicides, unintentionally launching a war on the soil. The result has been massive loss of topsoil over an area the size of Africa. And because the remaining soil is depleted and lifeless, our food contains fewer nutrients.

Koinonia Farm, a Christian community in southwest Georgia, began seventy-two years ago on an eroded and almost treeless piece of land. Our focus and passion is the soil, since healthy soil produces healthy food. We practice biological, regenerative farming, using none of the "-cides" (from the Latin *-cida*, meaning "a killer"); all organisms, even weeds, are important. To build organic matter, we apply compost teas, soil amendments such as molasses and gypsum, and bio-stimulants, and we spray beneficial bacteria, fungi, protozoa, and nematodes. Our goal is soil teeming with diverse life. According to research by the Rodale Institute, rebuilding the soil may even be part of the answer to climate change.

Since embracing this practice, we have seen remarkable growth of biodiversity not only in the soil, but on it and above it. The variety of bird species has dramatically increased. One Koinonia member recently counted more than fifteen types of butterflies on a single walk. Our cattle are grass-fed and serve the soil through a system called intensive grazing, and our chickens follow the cattle from sunup to sundown, sanitizing the land.

Back in 1957, local Ku Klux Klan members angered by Koinonia's multiracial membership sought to force the community to sell the land and move away. Koinonians refused to go. Founding member Clarence Jordan reflected on their decision:

> Fifteen years ago we went there and we bought that old, run-down, eroded piece of land. It was sick. There were gashes in it. It was sore and bleeding. I don't know whether you've ever walked over a piece of ground that could almost cry out to you and say, "Heal me, heal me!" I don't know whether you feel the closeness to the soil that I do. But when you fill in those old gullies and terrace the fields and you begin to feel the springiness of the sod beneath your feet and you see that old land come to life, and when you walk through a little old pine forest that you set out in little seedlings and now you see them reaching for the sky and hear the wind through them . . . Men say to you, "Why don't you sell it and move away?" They might as well ask you, "Why don't you sell your mother?" Somehow God has made us out of this old soil and we go back to it and we never lose its claim on us.

Surely the original soil from which humankind arose was rich and life-filled. At Koinonia, we are making every attempt to set the table for those coming after us. Life begets life.

Bren Dubay is a member of the Koinonia community in Americus, Georgia, founded in 1942 as a "demonstration plot for the kingdom of God." The community grows pecans, operates a bakery, and welcomes visitors. www.koinoniafarm.org

Carlton Murrell, *Thinking*, 1990 (Oil on Board)

JOHANN CHRISTOPH ARNOLD

Discovering Reverence

The Forgotten Virtue that Is the Key to
Educating Children

*A procession of angels passes before each human being wherever he goes,
proclaiming: Make way for the image of God!*

—RABBI JOSHUA BEN LEVI (Deut. Rabba 4, 4)

I N A SOCIETY overwhelmed by countless problems, the dangers to children are obvious: poverty, violence, neglect, disease, abuse, and countless other ills. But what can any one of us do to overcome them? In an essay on the question of social renewal, Hermann Hesse suggests that the first step is to recognize their root cause: our lack of reverence for life.

> All disrespect, all irreverence, all hardheartedness, all contempt is nothing else than killing. And it is possible to kill not only what is in the present, but also that which is in the future. With just a little witty skepticism we can kill a good deal of the future in a child or young person. Life is waiting everywhere, flowering everywhere, but we only see a small part of it and trample much of it with our feet. [1]

Hesse touches on something that endangers children more than anything else in the world today. Irreverence for children pervades almost everything in a culture that glorifies sex and violence at the expense of innocence and gentleness. While no one is unaffected by this destructive bent, the greatest victims are children. Often it seems that they are not given the chance to grow up at all – they are thrown into adult life before their hearts are able to distinguish between what is good and what is glamorous. They end up copying the worst of adult behavior without knowing what they are doing. They may not be grown up, but they are no longer truly children either.

Diane Levin, a child advocate, highlights the source of much of this contamination:

> A decline in social skills can be amplified when combined with the media's message of violence, aggression, and mean-spirited behavior as well as sex, sexualization, and focus on appearance. The media culture frequently supports a stereotypical view that, for girls, the basis of relationships is how they look and the things they have, rather than their connection to others. And media culture teaches boys to judge themselves and one another based on how strong, independent, and ready to fight they are, not by their positive connection with others. In a sense, both boys and girls are made into objects. Objectification of self and others makes it much easier to act in mean and uncaring ways in relationships. [2]

When children sense that they are being treated as objects, why shouldn't they respond accordingly? It's as if all that is wonderful, unique, and miraculous in each life is brought down to the lowest common denominator: gender. Without a clear sense of self, they can have no appreciation of who they are or how they came into being. Then they are fed a new, perverse interpretation of what it means to be male or female.

This promotes the formation of cliques, which often leads to bullying. Boys tend to take on a false manliness, a macho swagger that hides (at least from themselves) collective cowardice. Girls' cliques can be equally damaging in their exclusiveness and cruel pressure to

Johann Christoph Arnold is senior pastor of the Bruderhof and the author of twelve books, including Their Name Is Today: Reclaiming Childhood in a Hostile World, *(Plough, November 2014). This article is taken from that book.* www.theirnameistoday.com

conform. Worse, these children are prematurely burdened with adult sexuality.

So many features of our "advanced civilization" seem bent on destroying the spirit of childhood. Be it materialism, over-dependence on prescription drugs, standardized testing, too much technology, or the debased sensationalism that passes for entertainment, all of it harms children.

I believe that at birth, all children bear the stamp of their Creator. Their purity and innocence is a great gift. Once it has been lost, it cannot be replaced. All the more, it must be guarded as a treasure which no one has a right to destroy.

Our response upon encountering a child must be nothing less than reverence. Perhaps because the word sounds old-fashioned, its true meaning has been blurred. Reverence is more than just love. It includes an appreciation for the qualities children possess (and which we ourselves have lost), a readiness to rediscover their value, and the humility to learn from them.

Reverence is also an attitude of deep respect, as expressed by the following words of my grandfather Eberhard Arnold, a theologian and educator:

"It is children who lead us to the truth. We are not worthy to educate even one of them. Our lips are unclean; our dedication is not wholehearted. Our truthfulness is partial; our love divided. Our kindness is not without motives. We ourselves are not yet free of lovelessness, possessiveness, and selfishness. Only sages and saints – only those who stand as children before God – are really fit to live and work with children."[3]

Understanding reverence can change our perception of the world and our task in it. This simple word can help us keep our own lives clear of entanglements that may try to drag us down. With the knowledge that a young audience is watching our every move, we can be models of integrity and respect. We can dress in a manner that expresses our inner worth, instead of degrading it. Instead of bombarding young children with explicit information about sexuality and reproduction, we can let them grow at their own pace into an understanding of what it means to be a human being, and answer questions honestly and simply as they arise.

We can model healthy relationships. I learned the importance of this from my own parents, who could disagree with each other quite openly, but would end the debate with a laugh and a hug. I saw that my father was not ashamed to show tenderness and that my mother's gentle guidance was backed up with enormous courage. Their marriage, built on faithfulness and respect, was an example to all who knew them.

Once we have reverence for every life, we will also have compassion, and teach others its

Pierre-Auguste Renoir, *Margot Berard*

Once we have reverence for every life, we will also have compassion, and teach others its value.

value. Even the most hardened and distant child can learn empathy, and it is amazing to watch it happen. That's what Mary Gordon discovered when she founded Roots of Empathy, a program that brings babies into classrooms, with remarkable effects in reduced bullying. She writes:

"Darren was the oldest child I ever saw in a Roots of Empathy class. He was in eighth grade and had been held back twice. He was two years older than everyone else and already starting to grow a beard. I knew his story: his mother had been murdered in front of his eyes when he was four years old, and he had lived in a succession of foster homes ever since. Darren looked menacing because he wanted us to know he was tough: his head was shaved except for a ponytail at the top and he had a tattoo on the back of his head.

"The instructor of the Roots of Empathy program was explaining to the class about differences in temperament. She invited the young mother who was visiting the class with Evan, her six-month-old baby, to share her thoughts about her baby's temperament. Joining in the discussion, the mother told the class how Evan liked to face outwards when he was in the infant carrier, how he didn't want to cuddle into her, and how she wished he was a more cuddly baby. As the class ended, the mother asked if anyone wanted to try on the carrier, which was green and trimmed with pink brocade.

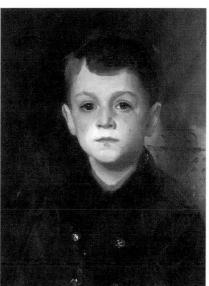

John Singer Sargent, detail, *Portrait of Lancelot Allen*

It is children who lead us to the truth. We are not worthy to educate even one of them.

"To everyone's surprise, Darren offered to try it, and as the other students scrambled to get ready for lunch, he strapped it on. Then he asked if he could put Evan in. The mother was a little apprehensive, but she handed him the baby, and he put Evan in, facing towards his chest. That wise little baby snuggled right in, and Darren took him into a quiet corner and rocked back and forth with the baby in his arms for several minutes. Finally, he came back to where the mother and instructor were waiting and asked: 'If nobody has ever loved you, do you think you could still be a good father?'

"A seed has been sown here. This boy, who has seen things no child should see, whose young life has been marked by abandonment, who has struggled to adolescence with scarcely a memory of love, has seen a glimmer of hope. Through these moments of contact with the uncritical affection of the baby, a young man has caught an image of himself as a parent that runs counter to his loveless childhood. The baby may have changed the trajectory of this youth's future by allowing him to see the humanity in himself."[4]

Today even small children hear about many threatening events, from terrorism and warfare to global warming and widespread hunger. All this can make a child fearful. Here a child's simple faith in the power of good – that love and

The author and his wife, Verena, with their granddaughter, Stephanie Jean (September 3– October 5, 2008)

compassion are stronger than hate or indifference – can quickly transform this fear into confidence and a desire to do something for others. I have found this faith in children all over the world, regardless of their religion. But parents need to nurture it. When we tell our children that the God who made the world loves each of them personally, we give them a deep assurance that, whatever happens, they are never alone.

As a pastor, I believe that even though God and Jesus are "illegal" in public school classrooms, teachers should never be afraid to live out their faith, even if wordlessly, and let it guide their daily interactions with children. We can acknowledge and protect the spark of the eternal that lives in each of them, the unique soul that needs our reverence and respect, no matter how difficult or unhappy the child may be. Children's own faith should be respected and affirmed. If they believe that God sees everything, that their guardian angel watches over them, or that Jesus is their friend, this can help them withstand the pressures that flood our culture.

There's another sphere of life that must be brought to a child with great reverence. To me, the mystery of birth and death can only be expressed in terms of eternity. This is not only because of my upbringing, since my parents lived their faith more than they talked about it. Rather, it's because of the times in my own life when something far greater than words could clearly be sensed, through someone who never spoke a word. I have seen how even the shortest life can transform all those within its reach.

My little sister Marianne died when I was six. Our family had waited for her arrival with great eagerness. She was born after my mother went through a very difficult labor for over sixty hours and suffered near-fatal heart failure. It was miraculous that she survived delivery at the primitive village hospital in Paraguay. But the baby was critically ill, and only lived for twenty-four hours. Because we lived quite a distance from the hospital, and because I was only six, I was never able to see, touch, or hold my little sister. Still, I have felt this loss my entire life. Over time, it has become all the more important to me to remember that Marianne was – and is – a real part of my life and my family. Though she was here on this earth for only one day, she will always be my sister.

Years later, I experienced this link with heaven even more clearly through another child, my granddaughter Stephanie Jean, who will remain in my heart for the rest of my life. When Stephanie was born, we knew right away that she was a very special child with severe abnormalities. She was diagnosed with Trisomy 13, a genetic disorder characterized by a short life expectancy. Most infants born with this disorder die within a few days.

Stephanie had three sisters and one brother. They struggled to understand that their parents were not going to bring home the healthy baby they all had longed for, but an extremely disabled child who would not live long. We prayed constantly that God's will might be done in her life, and that we would grasp the meaning of her birth.

As grandparents, we experienced the wonder of holding her almost daily. Stephanie lived for five weeks, and when the time came, died peacefully. At her funeral, we could not believe how many people attended. They had all heard of her birth and diagnosis, and it affected them deeply. They wanted to participate in this last expression of love for a small child who somehow belonged to everyone.

People came from all over the neighborhood and beyond: construction workers, her siblings' teachers and classmates, the county executive, the local sheriff, and others from the law enforcement community. When the earth was shoveled by hand into her little grave, these friends and neighbors all wanted to take a turn, in an unforgettable gesture of reverence. It was remarkable how in such a short time this little girl had touched and influenced the lives of so many people.

My granddaughter has not been forgotten. She is like a ray of light from heaven that continues to work in people and change their lives. My wife and I still thank God that he gave her to our family, and to everyone else she met.

There are many others like Stephanie. To me, every child is part of God's plan, and he does not make mistakes. When a child is disabled, her life takes on special significance. Whenever we encounter such children, we need to pay attention. They have amazing things to teach us about unconditional trust and love.

At a time when people are often assessed in terms of their worth, intelligence, or attractiveness, there are many who are not wanted or appreciated. But if we truly love children, we will welcome them all. Jesus says, "Whoever welcomes one such child in my name welcomes me."

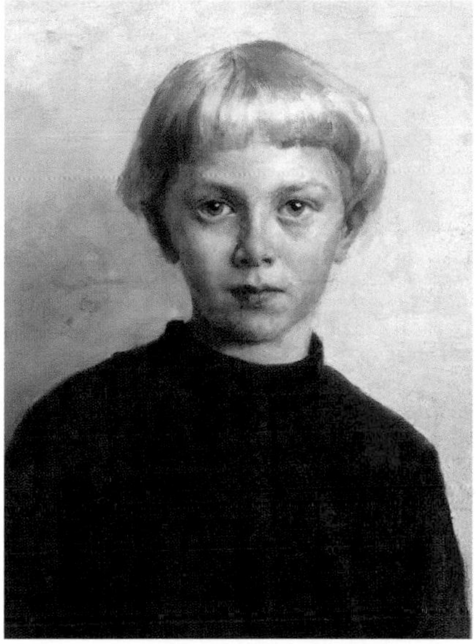

Konstantin Makovsky,
detail, *Portrait of the Boy*

Every child is part of God's plan, and he does not make mistakes.

As a teenager I was privileged several times to meet Dorothy Day, the legendary pacifist who founded the Catholic Worker, and to participate in some thought-provoking discussions. In her bohemian days, Dorothy had had an abortion, but several years later gave birth to her daughter Tamar, and was moved to write, "Even the most hardened, the most irreverent, is awed by the stupendous fact of creation. No matter how cynically or casually the worldly may treat the birth of a child, it remains spiritually and physically a tremendous event."[5] Tamar's birth changed her mother's life, and indeed, every child has such transformative power. This is just as true of a stillborn baby, or a child who dies young.

Whether or not we believe in a loving God, we can all show love and respect toward the children in our care. This will in turn awaken their own inborn sense of reverence – both for themselves as unique individuals, and for others, just as precious and distinctive. Only then will they truly understand their purpose and responsibility in the world.

1 Herman Hesse, *Vivos Voco*, March 1919, as quoted in Eberhard Arnold, *Salt and Light* (Plough, 1997), 48.

2 Diane Levin, *Beyond Remote-Controlled Childhood: Teaching Young Children in the Media Age* (NAEYC, 2013), 16, 37.

3 Eberhard Arnold, *Children's Education in Community* (Plough, 1976), 13–14.

4 Gordon, Mary, *Roots of Empathy: Changing the World, Child by Child* (Thomas Allen, 2005), 5–6.

5 Dorothy Day, *Dorothy Day: Meditations*, comp. Stanley Vishnewski (Newman, 1970), 10.

Schooling Me, the Surgeon

What I've Learned from Children with Disabilities

An Interview with Joseph Dutkowsky, MD

Joseph Dutkowsky is an orthopedic surgeon who specializes in treating children with disabilities such as cerebral palsy, spinal bifida, and muscular dystrophy; he divides his time between Columbia University in Manhattan and Cooperstown in upstate New York. Recently profiled in the New York Times *and on PBS, he stands out as a rare public example of someone whose faith infuses his practice of medicine.* Plough *recently caught up with him on the road between jobs.*

Plough: *What drew you to working with children with disabilities, and what keeps you at it now?*

Dr. Dutkowsky: Well, the truth is I haven't the foggiest notion what drew me to this work, but I can tell you how it happened. I was working on the West Coast for an aerospace company analyzing nuclear-weapons testing data and decided instead to apply to medical school. I wrote that I wanted to take some of this aerospace technology that was being employed to blow people up and use it to help people with disabilities, particularly children. I have no idea why I wrote that, but I did and it launched my vocation. It's the best job in the world.

You've said that when you stand before a child with disabilities you feel as though you are standing in the presence of God. Can you explain what you mean?

One of the things I have learned working with people with disabilities is that they live closer to the cross than the rest of us. They carry their disabilities all the time. They don't get a day off. They don't get a minute off. People with spasticity or athetosis feel it every day. People with Down syndrome have it wherever they go. And their disabilities are just as real and just as physical as the wounds on Jesus' hands and feet or the spear mark in his side that Thomas put his hand into. And so I find they bring me closer to the cross. They feel it; they sense it; they're part of it more than I am. I sometimes have to think my way there, whereas they simply guide me – they take me by the hand and bring me there. When you are there with them you are next to the resurrected Christ. That is the revealed glory of God.

You recently spoke to the Catholic Medical Association about the development of a modern form of eugenics, commenting, "Functional eugenics has now permeated our culture to a level of acceptance never achieved before." How do you account for this insidious trend?

There was a time, twenty to thirty years ago, when we really thought special education was important. It was a priority for us as a society; we passed laws, we appropriated funds, and we talked about it in depth. Now we think we cannot afford it. It has become almost exclusively an economic issue. And when you take the money away, all the other arguments – the cultural and social arguments – have no depth. It's like walking into the ocean up to your ankles: all that water, but only your feet get wet. This is what we're seeing with eugenics. The difference between the eugenics of a hundred years ago and today's functional eugenics is primarily economic. Our mentality today says if something isn't going to earn money for you (or worse, if it's going to cost you money), throw it away. This approach is bad enough if we're talking about coffee machines or cars. But it's gotten so bad that now we treat people this way.

Dr. Jérôme Lejeune was the physician who first counted forty-seven chromosomes on a tissue sample from a person with Down syndrome. He was struck immediately with two competing realizations. One was that for the first time, there existed a scientific basis that could be used to improve the lives of people with Down syndrome. But the second was that society could use this discovery to subject these people to discrimination, segregation, and even extermination. He wrote, "I see only one way left to save them, and that is to cure them."

Photograph courtesy of Rifton Equipment

Sadly, we are seeing today a declining will to save these people, to give them our best.

What should be our response as people of faith?

Our response is to proclaim that life is the greatest gift we can possibly be given. Nobody can will their heart to beat even once. Every heartbeat is a gift from God and it means he's not done with you yet. The idea that we are going to put less value on another person's heartbeat because they are disabled or because they carry an incurable disease is anathema to us. Remember, when Jesus rose from the dead he restored life in God-made man! In the face of that gift, how can we denigrate the life of any other human being?

A few months ago on Twitter a user posted this comment: "I honestly don't know what I would do if I were pregnant with a kid with Down syndrome. Real ethical dilemma." Within moments the prominent British evolutionary biologist Richard Dawkins responded, "Abort it and try again. It would be immoral to bring it into the world if you have the choice." This prompted a firestorm of debate that was picked up by news outlets around the world. If you had the opportunity to speak directly to Mr. Dawkins, what would you say?

Well, the first thing I would ask him is how many evolutionary biologists are happy with what they are doing in the world right now. You see, studies have shown that over 95 percent of people with Down syndrome are happy with their lives. They are satisfied. They're enjoying life. They appreciate the people in their lives. They feel loved. I'd like to know the numbers for evolutionary biologists. I'd like to know the numbers for orthopedic surgeons. Find me a group of people in this country who are as satisfied with life and as happy as people with Down syndrome.

The second thing I would tell him is that there is a price to pay for ignorance. Our last century has been brutal, and the cause is largely ignorance. Dawkins needs to educate himself and gain some firsthand experience with people with Down syndrome. I followed this story as it unfolded, and I applaud the person who responded to Dawkins by inviting him to dinner to meet his two children with Down syndrome. Richard Dawkins should revisit this question after he's taken the time to meet a few of the people he's talking about.

A remark you made when PBS profiled you last year struck me: "Suffering is real, but sharing suffering is a gift." Could you elaborate?

Suffering is very real. We're afraid of it. We run from it. But it's there, and when we learn to share it with others we draw close to them. Through that, we learn about love. I can't manufacture love; love is a gift. It comes to you and through you from God. It's like the stained-glass windows in a chapel. When you go in there at night in the dark they don't show anything; but when the light comes through them you see the glory of the colors and the beauty of the images, and it stirs you and brings you hope and joy. It brings you closer to God. That's what sharing love is all about.

You know, I truly believe that if God is gracious enough to let me get to heaven I will recognize Jesus because his will be the only disabled body up there. The scripture says that when we arise we will be given new heavenly bodies. But scripture also clearly says that Jesus ascended to heaven with the body that hung on the cross, with the nail holes in his hands and feet and the spear hole in his side. He carried

> Find me a group of people who are as happy and satisfied with life as people with Down syndrome.

Photograph courtesy of Rifton Equipment

with him the wounds on his head from the crown of thorns, the battered body from an all-night whipping. All those wounds will be there, and that is how we are going to recognize him. That's why these people are always bringing me closer to Jesus, because that is how we will encounter him at the end of our lives.

You have spoken of your medical work as a ministry. But who is ministering whom?

Our culture is addicted to perfection. If you just get the right car, the right wife, the right job, everything will be okay. But it's a lie. And the culture of perfection is one of the most dangerous things we face today. None of us is perfect. I've got my scars, you've got yours. But people with disabilities have taught me to recognize my own imperfections and to accept them. And through that they have taught me to learn to love myself as I am. This is one of the toughest things people struggle with today. I think it helps explain much of the drug abuse, alcohol abuse, domestic abuse, and suicide we see today. People are unable to love themselves, so they strike out in other ways. People with disabilities show us the value in our own life. This is a beautiful thing they give us. And it's not just children with disabilities who teach us. You go into a nursing home and talk with the residents and you discover the same thing.

In speaking about your practice you've sometimes referred to "Grand Canyon moments." Can you give me an example?

In modern medicine, you're often jerked about in three directions at once. Your pager is going off, your secretary is calling, the administrator wants something or other, and you're madly trying to meet everyone's needs and then something like this will happen: I had a young woman in my office with cerebral palsy whose arms were all pulled up against her. She asked me for Botox injections on her arms. "I can do that," I told her. Botox for someone with spasticity and contractures helps relax the muscles. After I administered the injections she turned to me and said, "Thank you, doctor. You know why I asked you to do this?" I said, "No, why?" She looked at me and said, "So I could hug my mom." Right there everything else going on around me faded away. It's like you've turned around and you're standing on the edge of the

Grand Canyon looking out over this expanse that no words could ever describe. And you realize you are standing in the presence of the glory of God. And you say to yourself, "What did I do to deserve this?" I think it's God's way of telling me, "Hold on a minute. Let me tell you what's really important."

You've suggested that people with disabilities have something of great value to contribute to our society. What are we missing out on if we try to shield ourselves from the effects of disability?

God forbid, if we were to rid ourselves of our special-needs children we might as well just live in a black-and-white world instead of full color, because we would be taking away the beauty inherent to life. Get rid of the blue sky we're enjoying today. Get rid of the gorgeous fall colors we're seeing outside – just make them shades of grey. That's what we'd be doing. People with disabilities share amazing things with us. As I said, they live closer to the cross. They understand better. They know they have a disability and they don't try to be something they're not. People with Down syndrome know they have Down syndrome, they know they don't have your intellect. It's okay with them. They're happy where they are. They tell us to accept our own imperfections, our need for forgiveness, our need for redemption, our need for being recreated. Through this we become better people. We become more satisfied. We become more whole. What a wonderful thing to reach the end of your life and think, "I've had a chance in this life to become more whole because I have spent time with people with disabilities." ⤳

> **If God is gracious enough to let me get to heaven, I will recognize Jesus because his will be the only disabled body up there.**

Interview by Joe Keiderling on October 3, 2014. Watch the video on www.plough.com.

INSIGHTS
on Childhood

Victor Borisov
Musatov,
Boy Seated

Janusz Korczak How can we assure a child's life in the future, if we have not yet learned how to live consciously and responsibly in the present? Do not trample, hold in contempt, or sell the future into bondage. Do not stifle it, rush, or force it. Respect every single moment, as it will pass and will never again be repeated. After all, when tomorrow finally does arrive, we start waiting for the next tomorrow.

Janusz Korczak (1878–1942) was a Polish-Jewish teacher and doctor whose selfless devotion to orphans in the Warsaw Ghetto earned him the title "King of Children." In 1942, as the two hundred orphans under his care were loaded onto trains headed for the gas chambers of Treblinka, Korczak chose to accompany his charges on the ride that carried them to their deaths.

Rachel Carson What is the value of preserving and strengthening the sense of awe and wonder, this recognition of something beyond the boundaries of human existence? Is the exploration of the natural world just a pleasant way to pass the golden hours of childhood or is there something deeper? I am sure there is something much deeper, something lasting and significant. Those who dwell, as scientists or laymen, among the beauties and mysteries of the earth are never alone or weary of life. Whatever the vexations or concerns of their personal lives, their thoughts can find paths that lead to inner contentment and to renewed excitement in living. . . . There is symbolic as well as actual beauty in the migration of the birds, the ebb and flow of the tides, the folded bud ready for the spring. There is something infinitely healing in the repeated refrains of nature – the assurance that dawn comes after night, and spring after the winter.

Rachel Carson (1907–1964) may be best known for her 1962 book Silent Spring, *which helped launch the environmental movement. But her legacy to children is* The Sense of Wonder, *a celebration of earth's beauty.*

Mary McLeod Bethune Our children must never lose their zeal for building a better world. They must not be discouraged from aspiring toward greatness, for they are to be the leaders of tomorrow. Nor must they forget that the masses of our people are still underprivileged, ill-housed, impoverished, and victimized by discrimination. We have a powerful potential in our youth, and we must have the courage to change old ideas and practices so that we may direct their power toward good ends.

Mary McLeod Bethune (1875–1955), an educator and activist, was president of the National Association of Colored Women, founder of the National Council of Negro Women, and special advisor to President Roosevelt on minority affairs.

Sources: Janusz Korczak, *Loving Every Child: Wisdom for Parents* (Algonquin Books of Chapel Hill, 2007). Rachel Carson, *The Sense of Wonder* (Harper & Row, 1956). Mary McLeod Bethune, "My Last Will and Testament" (*Ebony Magazine*, 1955).

Sir John Everett Millais, *Christ in the House of His Parents (The Carpenter's Shop),* oil on canvas, Tate Gallery, London

What's the Point of a Christian Education?

Preparing Children for the Freedom – and Cost – of Discipleship

CHRISTIAAN ALTING VON GEUSAU

On a lonely desert road outside of the Jordanian capital Amman, Joseph Fadelle finds himself with a gun pointed at his chest by his uncle, who is flanked by Joseph's four angry younger brothers. They demand that Joseph reconvert to Islam and denounce Christ if he wishes to save his life and save his wife and children from dishonor and poverty. They promise to restore his former privileged status and wealth if he will take up his old name, return with them to Baghdad, and never again profess his Christian faith.

Joseph refuses. It's December 22, 2000, almost thirteen years since he found faith in

Jesus Christ through the help of Massoud, a simple Christian farmer from a village near Mosul. Massoud, with whom Joseph shared a barracks room during his military service, lived his Christian discipleship quietly but visibly: humble, patient, and, despite the verbal abuse he suffered from his roommate, always charitable and peaceful, even though he was almost twenty years Joseph's senior. This attitude ultimately led to friendship, and eventually to Joseph's conversion.

The trigger was indeed pulled on Joseph, but he miraculously survived the hail of bullets. He was left for dead at the side of the desert road and somehow made it to a hospital where he was treated for his wounds. He eventually made it to Europe and today lives with his wife and children in France. This true story, told by Joseph Fadelle himself in *The Price to Pay* (Ignatius Press, 2012) shows that even today Christian discipleship may mean risking – or losing – one's life for Christ. In areas of Iraq and Syria controlled by the Islamic State, Christians are literally losing their heads because of their faithfulness to Christ. They are experiencing what Jesus warned us of: "An hour is coming when those who kill you will think that by doing so they are offering worship to God" (John 16:2).

What does this harrowing story have to do with teaching discipleship to our children? Why would the suffering of Christians in faraway lands be important for parents and educators in countries where we do not (yet) find ourselves in such a dramatic situation? My wife and I have told the story of Joseph and Massoud to our children, and we also share with them news about persecuted Christians around the world, because we want them to know the reality of what it means to be a Christian in today's world. These stories teach a number of vital lessons.

Friendship

The first lesson is friendship. Joseph Fadelle found Christ through his military colleague Massoud, who understood and followed the only route to a life lived in truth: divine friendship and human friendship. Discipleship is first and foremost a personal relationship with Christ; this intimate friendship must become the foundation of our life. Through Christ, we will be led to friendship with our neighbor, at whose door Christ knocks too. Jesus tells us: "No one has greater love than this, to lay down one's life for one's friends. You are my friends if you do what I command you" (John 15:13–14). Massoud was willing to risk his life to guide Joseph patiently to the gospel.

Friendship with Jesus allows us to see people through his eyes and discover the longing and goodness of the soul of our neighbor. This is what happened to Massoud when he shared the gospel with Joseph in the Iraqi military barracks. In the most unlikely of places and circumstances, he was able to reach the heart of a man who showed every sign of hostility and prejudice toward him as a Christian.

Faithfulness

The second lesson is faithfulness. Massoud was faithful to the clear and recurring exhortation to discipleship in the Gospels: "Go therefore and make disciples of all nations, baptizing them in the name of the Father and of the Son and of the Holy Spirit, and teaching them to obey everything that I have commanded you" (Matt. 28:19–20). This exhortation is directed at every Christian, no matter when or where. Massoud

Dr. Christiaan W. J. M. Alting von Geusau is president and rector of the International Theological Institute in Vienna and founder and chairman of the Schola Thomas Morus in Baden bei Wien. His most recent book is Catholic Education in the West: Roots, Realities and Revival *(Acton Press, 2013). He is married with five children.* www.iti.ac.at

courageously answered this call in a context where this might have meant death. Not all of us are being asked for such a radical act of discipleship, but this example should remind us to remain faithful to our calling at all times, even when the tides of the times are against us. We must be ready to give our all – including our lives – in order to be faithful to our vocation, especially our calling to spread the gospel to all corners of the earth.

Pope Francis underlined this in his homily during a Mass celebrated for over three million youth from around the world gathered on Copacabana Beach in Rio de Janeiro in July 2013:

> Where does Jesus send us? There are no borders, no limits: he sends us to everyone. The gospel is for everyone, not just for some. It is not only for those who seem closer to us, more receptive, more welcoming. It is for everyone. Do not be afraid to go and to bring Christ into every area of life, to the fringes of society, even to those who seem farthest away, most indifferent. The Lord seeks all – he wants everyone to feel the warmth of his mercy and his love.

"Going," "teaching," "observing," and "all" are central words of Christ when he calls us to discipleship. These words make us realize that living the gospel cannot be a halfhearted affair, because it means faithfully going to all, teaching all, and observing all. Such faithfulness has a clarity that is refreshing and liberating; it should be our starting point for teaching Christian discipleship to our children and young people. It invites them to focus on the essential question as they develop their personality and prepare for their vocation in the world: "What does it mean to be human?"

Formation

This brings us to the third lesson: formation. To find out what it means to be human – a lifelong task – we need to learn, and teach our children, to see the world through the eyes of God. This is why dedicated study of scripture should be an integral part of every Christian's education. It was Massoud's knowledge of scripture that enabled him to reach Joseph and open up a whole new perspective to a hardened and blinded heart. When we learn to see through the eyes of God, we will understand the created order he gave us and our place in that order. We will learn what it means to be human. Few have expressed this better than Pope Benedict XVI:

> Charity calls the educator to recognize that the profound responsibility to lead the young to truth is nothing less than an act of love. Indeed, the dignity of education lies in fostering the true perfection and happiness of those to be educated. In practice "intellectual charity" upholds the essential unity of knowledge against the fragmentation which ensues when reason is detached from the pursuit of truth. (Address to Catholic educators on April 17, 2008 in Washington, DC)

As disciples, we must dedicate our life to the pursuit of truth. But we can only do so if our hearts and minds have been so formed that we are able to stand upright in a world that is utterly confused, a world that has become enslaved to its passions, to the trends of the day, and to the violence which ensues when faith is detached from reason, and reason is detached from faith. How else can we explain some of the extremes of our age: abject poverty, rising ideologically inspired violence, the sexualization of society, the killing of the unborn, and the breakdown of families? G. K. Chesterton rightly points out that Christian discipleship "is the only thing that frees a man from the degrading slavery of being a child of his age."

In my own case, I cannot thank my parents enough for refusing to allow my siblings and me to conform to the popular trends of our times. Instead, they immersed us in a profoundly Christian culture full of beauty and wisdom, resplendent with the unity of knowledge about which Benedict XVI speaks. This happened through regularly attending church, praying together as a family, reading good literature, playing and listening to classical music, and sitting down together for family meals, which became occasions for conversation about current events. We also learned about chastity and the sanctity of marriage, and how self-control and self-giving lead to profound freedom. All this allowed us children to be formed in the good, the beautiful, and the true; it freed us to shape our lives according to what we were meant to be, rather than what either our passions or the latest fashions might push us to be.

When in 2012 my wife and I founded a new high school, the Schola Thomas Morus, in our hometown in Austria, the school's founding principles were clear from the start. It was to be a school with a living faith, with formation in the classical virtues, and with a rigorous curriculum that teaches children how to think, how to understand, and thus how to learn. These are the necessary attributes for young men and women entering the world to take their place of responsibility and service for the good of society. They will succeed in this only if they have grasped the reality of the created order and accepted it, rather than wanting to manipulate it according to the ideology of the day.

Few saints have understood this better than Sir Thomas More, for whom our school is named. Thomas More lost his life for refusing to give in to the whims of his king and country in violation of God's order. As he put it in his last words before dying by the axe: "I die as the King's faithful servant, but God's first." His son-in-law reported that on one occasion he gave his children the following encouragement:

> If you live the time that no man will give you good counsel, nor no man will give you good example, when you shall see virtue punished

and vice rewarded, if you will then stand fast and firmly stick to God, upon pain of life, though you be but half good, God will allow you for whole good. (Quoted in William Roper, *The Life of Sir Thomas More*)

Following More's example, we must foster in children the desire to pursue the truth with a listening heart, one that applies reason and is guided by a living faith. Our families, our schools, and our churches should all be places where children receive this kind of formation – an education that sets all we learn and do in the light of Christ.

Freedom

This brings me back to Joseph and Massoud, whose most important lesson on Christian discipleship might all too easily be overlooked. It's a lesson taught as well by the increasing numbers of Iraqi and Syrian Christians, young and old, who are being told by fellow human beings to renounce their faith or else lose their lives by the sword. In the face of these threats, their answer is, "You can take everything from us, even our lives, but you cannot take away our faith in Jesus Christ." What Joseph and Massoud knew, and what the heroic Christian martyrs testify to today, is that our true home is in heaven, where a loving Father is waiting for us. This certainty is what gives a disciple of Christ such an inner freedom on his or her earthly journey. Such freedom is ultimately the greatest gift we can give our children.

Every Child Is a Thought of God

THE SECRET AT THE HEART OF EDUCATION

EBERHARD ARNOLD

When we receive a little child from God, a soul is entrusted to humankind from eternity. No matter how often this happens, each time it is a powerful event, something unbelievably great.

We love little children because Jesus loved them. And from him we know that the kingdom of God belongs to them – in fact, that the kingdom is nearer to them than to the millions of adults.

Seen in this light, education is no arbitrary molding of a child, as the unbelieving world imagines. We cannot shape or form our children however we like, according to our own preferences. If we are to serve them rightly, we will form them only according to the way God has already thought of them.

Every child is a thought of God. We can only perform the service of education when we understand the thought of God for each child – a thought that God has had in eternity, and still has, and will always have just for this child. This thought of God is the holy "So be it" for this child.

God knows what each child is intended to become. It is the task of the parents, the church, and the educators to help this child become just what he or she should be, in accordance with the original thought of God. Through a religious sensitivity, we must attain a vision of this thought of God, which is still apparently hidden, and must learn to understand it more clearly

Philipp Otto Runge, detail, *The Morning*

from moment to moment, from day to day, from year to year. Then the forming of the child will not be something we undertake ourselves; rather, our role will consist solely in assisting in the formation intended by God. That is the secret of this task.

It is the same in our relationship with every individual adult. We must see each human being just as he or she is intended in the heart of God, in the holy purpose of his "So be it." Above all, we must wish for each person that he or she is integrated into the ultimate thoughts of God, so that God's final will may be revealed among humankind: that is, the church and the kingdom of the complete unity of Jesus Christ.

We thus bear a crucial responsibility to live in reverence for the Holy Spirit. This is true for all aspects of the church's life, but it applies in an especially holy sense to the bringing up of children. Reverence for the Holy Spirit means reverence for the father, who is to represent Christ as the God-given head; reverence for the mother, who is to represent Christ in the likeness of Mary and the church; and reverence for the child and for the wonderful mystery of being a child and becoming a child.   ➥

Eberhard Arnold (1883–1935) was a German theologian and educator. These words are taken from remarks at the dedication of a newborn, September 30, 1934. Translated by Nicoline Maas. www.eberhardarnold.com

Kindergartners Are Human Beings

And Other Facts Often Forgotten in the Age of Common Core

JOAN ALMON

I once heard a wise professor of education remark to his class that behind every educational approach stands a picture of the human being. "But many of you," he said, "will teach for thirty years or more, and no one will ever ask you what image you hold – what picture of the human being shapes your education."

What image stands behind American education today? Is it a mechanistic picture or a human picture? The Common Core State Standards are rolling out in state after state, redefining much of American education. Designed to help students prepare for college and the workplace, they are also purported to cultivate creative and critical thinking and problem solving. While these are important goals, it is unlikely that the standards will advance them.

The very concept of standards is better suited to the world of machines and factories than to children and schools. When the phrase *Common Core standards* first started to circulate in educational circles, I did a web search for the term. The only entries I found were for building materials.

Standards are necessary when we want uniform products. But children are not meant to fit a single mold. While they have much in common, each is a unique individual, and education needs to build on both their commonality and their individuality. We have fallen into the trap of treating children as if they are small machines that can be calibrated according to our sense of timing. If a child today fails to develop at the pace prescribed by the standards, there are apt to be serious consequences – the child may repeat a grade, or enter

---

Joan Almon, a Waldorf early-childhood educator for over thirty years, is cofounder of the Alliance for Childhood, which seeks to give all children a healthy and creative childhood. With Ed Miller, she wrote the 2009 report Crisis in the Kindergarten: Why Children Need to Play in School. www.allianceforchildhood.org

Courtesy of Community Playthings

kindergarten goals heavily emphasize short-term gains, many of which disappear after a few years. In the end, we have arbitrarily created a new pathway of development for young children, and concretized it with official standards and high-stakes tests. Many teachers see how inappropriate this new pathway is, but do not have the freedom to make necessary changes.

As a result, children may unconsciously begin to think of themselves in mechanistic terms. They feel inferior to the computers they are taught to handle before they learn to handle themselves or the world around them. They hear us say that the brain is like a computer, but they don't realize that the brain came first and the computer is an imitation. They hear us praise artificial intelligence, but do not understand how pale it is compared to the human intelligence that combines heart and mind. We hand young children our phones and tablets, forgetting to offer them our lullabies and nursery rhymes. We should not be surprised, then, if they increasingly look to machines for comfort and companionship. Without realizing it, we are shaping children to fit a mechanized world, not raising them to inhabit a human world.

What do young children really need? From birth onwards, they carry a deep drive to grow and learn. They want to find their way in the world using their bodies, emotions, and minds. They have a sense of their own path of development, what they should do next, and how they should do it. How else does a one-year-old know it is time to walk or a two-year-old to speak? No one tells young children to do this. From deep within, they know what they need to master next, and they watch others doing it. Then they develop the ability to do it for themselves.

Children cannot become mature human beings by themselves. They experience our love and warmth as a cocoon that protects them from harm. They need us to set appropriate

special education classes, or her teachers may be penalized or even fired. It is hard to see how an education based on fixed standards and high-stakes testing can help children achieve their full humanity.

As an early-childhood educator I am most concerned about the Common Core standards for the kindergarten age, since these seem especially ill-matched to children's development. They require that over ninety skills be achieved by the end of the kindergarten year. Some of these skills are sensible enough, but many others are far better suited to later grades. To meet the standards, teachers increasingly rely on long periods of teacher-led instruction, worksheets, homework, and tests. As a result, they can provide little time or support for child-initiated play and hands-on exploration, both of which prepare children for an active, creative life.

The Common Core standards are said to be evidence-based, but the evidence for what is now expected from kindergartners is slim. The

boundaries and guidelines, yet give them as much freedom to explore as they can handle. They need us to be both strong and compassionate, people who understand the importance of living a life that is good and beautiful and true. And they need our faith in their ability to find their own way in life, so they can fulfill their own unique purpose. In short, they need us to strive to become full human beings, so we can help them do the same.

> **It's time to be grateful for every child who comes before us, and for the wonder of human life itself.**

What does it mean to be a full human being? It means that our whole nature is activated and integrated – our thinking, our feeling, and our willing. Individuals may be naturally more gifted in one area than another, but all of these elements are necessary for a full life. Being human means we have body, soul, and spirit, and we embrace the heavenly world as we do the earthly. We stand like a bridge between the two; our feet curve gently to touch the earth, and our heads reflect the dome of the sky. In between, our hearts reach out to one another.

Such a picture of humanity raises the question: where does a child come from before he or she rests in our arms? George MacDonald suggests an answer:

Where did you come from, baby dear?
Out of the everywhere into the here.

And William Wordsworth, in his poem *Ode: Intimations of Immortality*, reminds us that we come to earth "trailing clouds of glory. . . . Heaven lies about us in our infancy." We hold the newborn and sense her great journey. She is full of life's possibilities, like a bud ready to open, petal by petal. How can we think, a few years later, that all this glory can be reduced to a series of test scores? Education is caught in a great denial of what it means to be a full and integrated human being. It is time to be grateful for every child who comes before us, and for the wonder of human life itself. Wordsworth speaks of this gratitude in the closing lines of his *Ode*:

Thanks to the human heart by which we live,
Thanks to its tenderness, its joys, and fears,
To me the meanest flower that blows can give
Thoughts that do often lie too deep for tears.

Educating the Whole Child

Friedrich Fröbel   Protect the new generation; do not let them grow up into emptiness and nothingness, to the avoidance of good hard work, to introspection and analysis without deeds, or to mechanical actions without thought and consideration. Guide them away from the harmful chase after outer things and the damaging passion for distraction. . . . I would educate human beings who stand with their feet rooted in God's earth, whose heads reach even into heaven and there behold truth, in whose hearts are united both earth and heaven.

Friedrich Fröbel, who created the concept (and the name) of the kindergarten, was a nineteenth-century German educator (see page 6). He emphasized the value of teaching the "whole child" through active play, creativity, music, art, and hands-on learning. With his unique ability to interpret life through a child's experience, he paved the way for many successful efforts in education today, influencing John Dewey, Maria Montessori, and the Waldorf movement. www.froebelweb.org.

Fröbel's words opposite are from his book *The Education of Man*, quoted in J. C. Arnold, *Their Name Is Today* (Plough, 2014).

JONATHAN KOZOL

Charity Is No Substitute for Justice

What Do We Owe America's Children?

The stories of the black and Latino children in New York City that Jonathan Kozol tells in his latest book Fire in the Ashes *cannot be read with indifference. The author is no snapshot journalist, flitting in and out of lives with quick judgments; he approaches his subjects with an astute eye and an open heart. These painful, beautiful stories make us ask, "When did the system break? And what can we do about it?" Kozol reflects:*

The word "accountability" is very much in fashion now. Children in the inner cities, we are told, must be "held accountable" for their success or failure. But none of these children can be held accountable for choosing where they have been born or where they have led their childhood. Nor can they be blamed for the historic failings of their schools. Nor, of course, are any of these children responsible in any way at all for the massive unemployment, and the flight of businesses and industries, that have put so many young men on the corners of the streets with no useful purposes within their daily lives. . . .

The question might be reasonably asked: If all of these externally determined forces of discouragement had not been present when these kids were growing up, would some of them have fallen into turbulent and painful lives in any case, or forfeited their lives before they even grew into maturity? There's no way to know, but I suppose the answer would be yes. Unhealthy and self-destructive inclinations are not the "special illnesses" of young men and women who grow up in inner-city neighborhoods. I recall, from my father's sixty years of practicing psychiatry, that he treated many affluent young people who seemed "hell-bent," as he put it, "on finding any way they can to ruin their own lives," and some of them attempted suicide repeatedly.

But, for the children of a ghettoized community, the pre-existing context created by the social order cannot be lightly written off by cheap and facile language about "parental failings" or by the rhetoric of "personal responsibility," which is the last resort of scoundrels in the civic and political arena who will, it seems, go to any length to exculpate America for its sins against our poorest people.

The question of exceptionality needs to be dealt with here.

Pineapple lived in the Diego-Beekman housing and trudged up the street to P.S. 65. That was where she had the teacher she called "Mr. Camel," one of the seven unprepared instructors who came and went throughout her third- and fourth-grade years. Jeremy lived in a tower of decrepitude where he was robbed at knifepoint, and sometimes had to walk the stairs to get to his apartment when the elevator, as he put it, didn't "want to come" down to the lobby. He was fortunate to go to P.S. 30; but he was often beaten up and bullied when he was in middle school.

Yet both these children, as well as several of the others I was close to at St. Ann's [Episcopal Church in the South Bronx], rose above the problems and the perils of the neighborhood, finished their schooling in a healthy state of mind, went on to college, and are now envisioning the range of opportunities their education will allow. . . .

Photograph by Chris Arnade

Patience and Allan, in Bushwick, Brooklyn

The point I need to emphasize again is that all these children had unusual advantages. Someone intervened in every case, and with dramatic consequences. In Lara's situation, it was a devoted teacher in a failing middle school and, again, a teacher at an otherwise unsuccessful high school in New York who "spotted" her as a gifted student and gave her individual tutorial instruction that enabled her to have her choice of colleges. In Pineapple's case, and Jeremy's and Leonardo's, it was either Martha [Rev. Martha Overall of St. Ann's] or someone from outside the Bronx, or a group of people from outside New York City altogether, who shepherded these children into avenues of exit from the damage they'd already undergone, or would likely undergo, in the schools of the South Bronx. Other children from the Bronx and similar communities have been given access to good education through programs like A Better Chance, which serves children nationwide, or Prep-for-Prep, an institution in New York that looks for highly motivated students in minority communities and helps them gain admission to some of the most exclusive prep schools in the city.

All of this, however, depends upon the charitable inclinations of a school or philanthropic donors, and charity has never been a substitute, not in any amplitude, for systematic justice and systematic equity in public education. If any lesson may be learned . . . it is not that we should celebrate exceptionality of opportunity but that the public schools themselves in neighborhoods of widespread destitution ought to have the rich resources, small classes, and well-prepared and well-rewarded teachers that would enable us to give to every child the feast of learning that is now available to children of the poor only on the basis of a careful selectivity or by catching the attention of empathetic people like the pastor of a church or another grown-up whom they meet by chance. Charity and chance and narrow selectivity are not the way to educate the children of a genuine democracy.

From Jonathan Kozol, Fire in the Ashes: Twenty-Five Years Among the Poorest Children in America *(Crown, 2012; Broadway Books, 2013). Reprinted with permission.*

Digging Deeper

Must-Reads

The Sense of Wonder
Rachel Carson
(HarperCollins)

The Teacher Wars
A History of America's Most Embattled Profession
Dana Goldstein
(Doubleday)

The King of Children
The Life and Death of Janusz Korczak
Betty Jean Lifton
(St. Martin's Press)

Recommended

The Age of Opportunity
Lessons from the New Science of Adolescence
Laurence Steinberg
(Houghton Mifflin Harcourt)

Getting Schooled
The Reeducation of an American Teacher
Garret Keizer
(Metropolitan Books)

Simplicity Parenting
Using the Extraordinary Power of Less to Raise Calmer, Happier and More Secure Kids
Kim John Payne
(Ballantine Books)

Bookstores boast an intimidating array of titles on children, education, and parenting. Here are some outstanding titles that will put limited time to good use:

Must-Reads: Rachel Carson, the environmentalist pioneer, wrote *The Sense of Wonder* toward the end of her life. Originally an essay titled "Help Your Child to Wonder," her spare, exquisite prose invites you to a ramble along a northern shore and through the wet Maine woodlands in spring. Luminous photographs show grass blades and tide pools through a child's eyes, while the text guides the reader to recover a sense of mystery and awe, to be shared – in turn – with the next generation.

Dana Goldstein's *The Teacher Wars: A History of America's Most Embattled Profession* reminds us that we ignore history at our peril. How many policymakers know that requiring children to take standardized tests, with results tied to teachers' job security, is an approach that has failed before? The book is full of such insights, taking the reader from the launch of the teacher-union movement, to the rise of community control, to the corporate takeover of education. When do teachers teach well? When they're supported and mentored by experienced colleagues who want them to succeed. When have American children excelled at learning? When their needs were addressed beyond the classroom.

The King of Children: The Life and Death of Janusz Korczak, by Betty Jean Lifton, belongs on any educator's bookshelf. We may wonder at the courage of a man who, when he could no longer protect the orphans in his care, chose to accompany them to face death together in Treblinka. But what of the life they shared before? What forces shaped him into a father of two hundred? "You do not leave sick children in the night. And you do not leave children at a time like this."

Recommended: In *The Age of Opportunity: Lessons from the New Science of Adolescence*, Laurence Steinberg, a developmental psychologist, argues that adolescence is a stage just as crucial as years zero to three. Adolescents are undergoing the last life phase when the brain remains malleable; it's a time of enormous opportunity, but also great risk. (In the United States, a sixth of adolescents are obese, a fifth of high-school-age boys are on anti-ADHD prescription drugs, and nearly a third of young women get pregnant before turning twenty.) The author first reviews findings from recent science, then offers practical advice to parents, educators, and policymakers. He emphasizes: "The most important contributor to wellbeing in adolescence is strong self-control." The good news? Self-discipline can be taught – if adults provide a supportive and positive environment.

Garret Keizer's *Getting Schooled: The Reeducation of an American Teacher* is a memoir of a high-school teacher who retires to pursue a writing career, then returns to teaching fifteen years later. Keizer's prose is deft, incisive, and humorous – even when he's inveighing against threats to real learning posed by standardized testing and ostensibly time-saving technology. He demands excellence, but cares enough to track a poor performance back to the hardships a student might face in her home life. If you're disillusioned by the political bickering over education, visit Mr. Keizer's classroom via this book.

Parents will find welcome encouragement in Kim John Payne's *Simplicity Parenting: Using the Extraordinary Power of Less to Raise Calmer, Happier and More Secure Kids*. It's hard to disagree with the title, but when it comes to taking action on it, the apparent enormity of the project may be daunting. This matter-of-fact handbook takes the time to explain why simplicity is worth the effort. ➤   *The Editors*

VIEWPOINT

Should Christians Abandon Public Schools?

CATHERINE MCNIEL

Last September, after my sons boarded the bus for a new year at our local public school, I read two articles that might make any parent question the decision to entrust a child to the public-school system. The first, in a local newspaper, documented the growing levels of poverty in schools in the suburbs of Chicago. The district with the biggest increase in poverty is the one in which my children are enrolled. No less than 76 percent of district students now come from low-income homes; many arrive at school hungry, and test scores are falling.

In the second article, Al Mohler, president of Southern Baptist Theological Seminary, asked Christian parents, "Is public education even an option anymore?" Writing for *Answers* magazine, he outlined various ideological problems, concluding that "for Christians who take the Christian worldview seriously and who understand the issues at stake, the answer is increasingly no."

Clearly, public schools can be troubled places. Accordingly, it's no surprise that the Christian consensus seems to side with Mohler; a quick online search yields an immediate harvest of articles imploring Christians to remove their children from public education. And when I meet people in town who share my faith and education, they often confess they never seriously considered enrolling their children in the local schools. The prevailing wisdom is that private or homeschool options are the best choice, that the extra investment of time and money allows us to put our children first, rooting them into the kingdom of God.

But what about the children who are left behind, in increasingly darker places as each Christian light is removed? Should the Christian response be to abandon troubled public schools – or should our answer rather be to infiltrate them?

Our family moved to this Chicago suburb after perceiving God's nudge to invest in his

Choosing public education is my Christian act of hope, justice, and redemption.

kingdom in this specific place. We want what every human wants – shelter, community, and security. But as followers of Christ we are called to something else as well: we are to be salt and light, representing his kingdom here and now.

Enrolling our children in the public school system is central to our life in this under-resourced, diverse community. Before moving here we did our homework, poring over the district's educational scorecards and demographic makeup. I'll admit I was concerned and burdened by the challenges associated with the poverty and often-complicated immigration situations in our new neighborhood. I understand why so many families seek other options. But when I visit our sons' elementary school and see the at-risk, English-as-a-second-language, first-generation American children working hard to make their way, I think of all the resources that are lost through educational white flight. My heart aches each time I meet a strong Christian family whose talents, resources, and faith will never intersect with the children in our public schools – including my own children. When I hear the well-intentioned advice, "If you move there, don't send your kids to the public school," my heart cries, "But that's where we need you!"

All the same, must I sacrifice my child for this cause? I feel the question deeply, and I am not suggesting we send our children out as little missionaries. Rather, I am calling for entire families and churches to flood the schools together. With the Body of Christ permeating these places, we would no longer have to choose between our children and our community. As the prophet Jeremiah proclaimed, "Seek the peace and prosperity of the city to which I have carried you into exile. Pray to the Lord for it, because if it prospers, you too will prosper" (Jer. 29:7). In this way, our children will learn to follow Christ, to bring him to the world, to live focused on others, and to understand other cultures. Supported by their parents and churches,

they will learn these life skills in our public schools.

After all, the demographics of our neighborhoods are not as impoverished as those of the school system. When families pull their children out of public school, they deprive that school of their resources and energy, prompting more families to opt out. Meanwhile, families with fewer resources have no option but to stay. Soon, districts with challenges and resources become simply districts with challenges. We should reverse this demographic spiral. If we flood instead of flee, we could impact these schools for the common good and the glory of God.

Choosing public education – even in a troubled school district – is my Christian act of hope, justice, and redemption. I choose public school not because I don't care, but as a commitment to care and invest even more. My husband and I see this as a kingdom-building opportunity, in our own small way adding what we have to the wellbeing of the city. And we are not alone – beyond the discouraging statistics and failing test scores we have found committed teachers, administrators, and parents working together to make a difference. God is always found working in even the darkest of places.

Jesus left his privilege to become one of us and to serve us. He was not afraid to get his hands dirty, not scared off by temptation or danger. If we follow him we must count the cost and pick up our cross, forsaking privilege for the sake of service. He implores us to put our light on a lampstand and not under a basket. By withdrawing from public schools, Christians have dimmed the light in places that desperately need it, clustering instead under the protective cover of our homes and churches.

In his book *Neighborhood Mapping,* John Fuder implores churches to serve their neighborhoods by becoming genuine, credible members of the community. "We can choose to remove our children from the 'bad' schools to enroll them in better, safer schools. But . . . God calls us to set aside our privilege and truly reside among those who have nothing, following Christ's model." The church has not adequately wrestled with the community-wide implications of our private decisions on how to educate our children. Where our children and treasure are, there our hearts will be also. When our hearts, children, and finances are mingled with our neighbors' to such a degree that we can only win if they win, we are following Christ's teaching.

Because the Christian message is life-changing in its power, and because our country's children are at stake, let's acknowledge the problems and respond with infiltration rather than abandonment. Let's seek not only to raise our own children to know Christ, but to follow him in seeking the redemption and peace of the city, to infuse his creation with salt and light and new life, and to place a light upon a hill.

Catherine McNiel serves alongside her husband in a community-based ministry in greater Chicago while caring for three kids, two jobs, and one enormous garden. She is a member of the Redbud Writers Guild. www.catherinemcniel.com

Why I Homeschool

PAISLEY HILLEGEIST

I thank God for the opportunity to homeschool my children. I am often asked: Why, when the local schools are so good, do we homeschool? Here are some of our reasons:

- We have the freedom to pray, read the Word of God, and discuss spiritual issues with our children as they come up throughout the day.

- Our curriculum is highly individualized. Every child gets one-on-one time with his or her teacher daily.

- Our children are not regularly exposed to drugs, alcohol, or sexual promiscuity. When we see it in public we are able to discuss it.

- We have opportunities to share our faith with others outside of the pressures of the school culture, with its cliques and bullying.

- We learn life skills together. How do you balance a checkbook? Mail a package? Do the laundry? Cook? Shop for the best deals? Build a chicken coop? Butcher turkeys? All this is part of our classroom.

- We have the time to pursue a Christian approach to relationships. Reconciliation and love are at the heart of our school day. Character comes first.

Historically, homeschooling has been the norm. Jesus would have been primarily taught at home. Most of our country's founding fathers were home-educated. In fact, only in the last two hundred years have people considered letting the state school their children. My children have been entrusted to me by God for a short while. Jesus said, "Render therefore unto Caesar the things which are Caesar's; and unto God the things that are God's" (Matt. 22:21 KJV). My kids belong to God, not to the state.

That said, we have not forgotten the children in our local school system. Nor are we trying to keep apart from the community. We have been involved, as a family, in afterschool programs such as theater groups. The children and I sing for residents of a retirement home and hand out food with the local food bank. Being homeschoolers does not mean that we drop out of the world. On the contrary, we've found that homeschooling frees our calendar to better serve, and to be involved in ways we never could if we were tied to a public-school schedule.

I respect and admire people who involve themselves in the local schools as a part of their ministry and outreach. My husband was a high-school math teacher in the barrios of East LA during the first part of our marriage. We met because we both shared a passion for working with the younger brothers and sisters of gang members and introducing them to Jesus.

We each walk our own path with Jesus. He may call some to homeschool, some not. But I believe with all my heart that the most powerful good I can bring to my community is to raise my kids in the way that will best help them to become the men and women that God has created them to be. That is why we homeschool.

Paisley Hillegeist and her husband Jon live in Connecticut and have homeschooled their three children, ages 14, 11, and 9, from the start.

From Getty Images, © Cultura / Jamie Kingham

GLENN T. STANTON

Why Dads Matter
And Moms Don't Toss Babies

In the passenger lounge of the Kansas City airport some years ago, I saw the most amazing thing: an infant flying up above a dividing wall, levitating for just a second, then dropping back down behind the wall. I couldn't look away; it happened again. And again, and again. I surmised one of two things. Either they have flying babies in Kansas City, or this baby was being tossed a couple of feet above head height by someone. And dollars to donuts, it was bound to be a father or grandfather doing the tossing.

I walked around a corner in order to see the event in full and sure enough, it was a "good ol' boy" American father doing the throwing, with baby loving every bit of it. Not by coincidence, mom was nowhere in sight.

On a recent trip to Asia, I turned on Chinese television, not able to understand a word. But I did understand what I saw in a commercial, and I saw the same thing happening in parks as I walked to my meetings. Fathers and grandpas were throwing their little ones into the air, to the children's immense delight and happiness (assuming that giggles have the same meaning across cultures). Apparently, this startling dad behavior is universal.

Consider this from the perspective of the baby, for whom the challenge of trying to figure out this interesting world is a full-time job.

Glenn T. Stanton's most recent book is Loving My (LGBT) Neighbor: Being Friends in Grace and Truth *(Moody Publishers, 2014).*

Every baby who has ever taken flight in such a way learned an essential life lesson. I call it the "scary world–safe world" experience.

When a baby – boy or girl – is thrown into the air the first few times, what does he or she do? You know, because you've seen it yourself, and in fact likely experienced it yourself way back when. The children gasp and hold their breath, eyes wide as quarters. With my children, I've often caused and seen that look of sheer terror.

First lesson learned? The child is realizing that the world is a scary place. (This is not a lesson he or she is likely to learn from mom, because moms are not into scaring their children; usually they are the comforters.) But just as quickly as the child feels that fear coming, gravity kicks in and he or she always comes back down, safely into the strong hands of dad.

Second lesson learned? The child learns the world can be a safe place in dad's hands. He or she experiences two very raw and deeply instructive human emotions. At one point, the child's whole being screams out, "Holy cannoli, this world is a dang scary place and I can't seem to trust anyone to take care of me!" Then, a split second later, the child feels, "Oh . . . good, now the world is safe and dad is there for me."

As babies, most of us have gone from being scared poop-less to giggling hysterically and begging for more. And almost always it was a male – a father, uncle, grandfather, family friend – who provided this experience, satisfying the same inborn desire that fuels the thrill-ride industry. But unlike roller coaster rides, this process is more than merely fun. It teaches the child that while scary things will come in life, you can count on dad to take care of you. This builds both confidence and comfort.

Mom is different. She mostly doesn't feel compelled to throw babies, but rather to hold them close, offering a different kind of security. Mom's way of comforting is essential, but it's also less likely to build confidence – it doesn't force the child out of his or her comfort zone. Confidence comes from taking risks and recovering safely from them. Dad's work.

A sad story told to me by a friend – who is a professional counselor – illustrates this truth poignantly. One of his adult clients was seeing him about his lifelong struggle to trust others. The client told how when he was a boy, his father played with him one day, having him jump off the porch steps and into his arms. With each jump, his dad would take a step back, forcing the boy to jump farther and harder. With each jump, the boy was learning that he could do it – he could take chances and succeed in hitting the mark, his dad's arms. When the father was a considerable distance from the porch, he encouraged the boy to give it all he had: "Jump one more time!" When he was in mid-air, the father stepped back a few steps, allowing his son to land right on his little face on the concrete walkway. In that instant, the boy's perception of the world changed dramatically, for life. He was hurt, crying, and terribly shaken, but the inward damage was much greater. He looked up at his father with an expression that screamed, "Why did you do that?" The dad looked sternly at the boy and said, "Just a little lesson, son. *Never* trust anyone."

And that is exactly what the boy grew up to do. His inability to trust others plagued him well into late adulthood.

Fathers who challenge their children to take risks while keeping them safe give them an irreplaceable gift. They encourage their children to push themselves, to climb higher, to run faster, to throw harder, to not give up on a problem, to move beyond fear. Moms, meanwhile, teach caution: "Please be careful. Not so high!" Children need both lessons.

Even in an age when we claim to have evolved beyond narrow gender stereotypes, fathers know their children need them. A

Good fathers challenge their children to take risks while keeping them safe.

Both a man and a woman are required for the creation of a new child, and both are needed for rearing that child.

national newspaper featured an experimental parenting co-op of four homosexual adults: two lesbians, their sperm-donor friend, and his gay partner. The foursome had one child and were expecting another. The interviewing journalist asked them whether, given their unique parenting arrangement, they ever had conflicts on how to raise the three-year-old child. The sperm-donor father spoke up, saying he believed the biological mother had a tendency to pamper the little boy too much. "When he falls down," he explained, "she wants to rush over and make sure he is okay. I know he will be fine." He wanted his boy to learn to trust in his own ability to solve his own problems – a crucial part of growing up. Like most dads, he was not as inclined as mom to provide an immediate answer, preferring to hold back and let the child figure it out.

In this instance, however, when the journalist probed how the four adults resolved such disagreements, the father sheepishly explained that since he was not a legal parent he just kept quiet. As a result of his silence, this child is missing out on a vital life experience. What's more, this man knows that the boy is being robbed of something important, thanks to a fathering nature that still exists regardless of any attempt to transcend seemingly old-fashioned male and female roles.

Self-Control

The benefits that a mother and a father can provide their children extend to learning self-control. Consider roughhousing. Moms often teach self-control by setting absolute rules on wild behavior in the house, with slightly less rigid rules applying outdoors. This is good. Children need to learn that there are not only an inside voice and an outside voice, but also inside and outside behaviors.

Fathers, however, are more likely to rough it up both in and outside the house. And when they wrestle with their children, the little ones are likely to get so intoxicated with the excitement that they will take it up a notch to increase the buzz. "It's all fun and games till someone loses an eye" – but with dad, that's only true up to a point. The fun stops quickly when he catches a little swinging foot or fist solidly in the daddy zone. Generally, this is the moment when dad initiates a firm talk about self-control. Usually it only takes a couple of such instances before junior gets the message. Boys with a good dad learn how to be physical while keeping proper self-control and considering others.

Dads and Pro-Social Behavior

Is there any community that is proud of its high gang activity? Is there any community that mourns its low teen-pregnancy rate and wishes that its young ladies would get out there more and mix it up? Moms and dads teach their sons and daughters universal virtues to combat these problems, but in different ways.

Boys generally have a naturally high level of aggression. They like to break things, rule them, show others who's boss. Every boy in every culture must learn how to manage this natural male aggression in socially constructive ways. Boys typically do so by receiving correction, acceptance, and encouragement from older men – whether through sports, in the military, by going hunting, or by building things that benefit others.

When a boy goes over the top – driving too fast, burning things, being aggressive toward others – the men, starting with dad, step in and tell him to bring it down a notch. On the other hand, if the boy is reticent or timid, the men will throw him into the middle of the action. In either scenario, the youngster eventually earns the respect and acceptance of the men around him. When a boy misses out on this because there is no dad to help him navigate through the

Photograph by Lucy Clement

curious world of the male, he may turn either hyperviolent or terribly passive.

Too often, the result is gangs. Gang members typically don't have a father to guide them and to let them know that they measure up and can respect themselves. In response, these boys make sure the world recognizes them – by engaging in conscienceless physical violence, intimidation, sexual dominance and opportunism, and foolish risk-taking. Mothers can help curb such behavior by their disapproval and broken hearts, but the most powerful and direct cure is an involved dad.

Girls can be violent as well, and they too will desire the attention of the opposite sex. Young women who have been mothered and fathered well are dramatically less likely to become victims of their own emotions and sexuality. A young girl who is sexually healthy is one who has learned what it's like to be properly loved and cared for by a good man. She learns this first and foremost from her father. To such a girl, a man is not a mystery, and so she is less likely to fall for the manipulative advances of opportunistic males.

Dads and Language Development

Even in terms of language ability, mothers and fathers make different yet essential contributions to a child's development. A mom is more likely to connect verbally with her children at their own level, using words, phrases, and tones of voice that allow for immediate understanding. Dad's way is different, less tailored to the child's own speech and often seemingly less successful. I often noticed this when our children were young. Our child would fall, skin her leg, and start crying. Mom would say, "My goodness, you have a terrible boo-boo." Dad's response might be: "That's quite an abrasion, kid." Dad's way provides a vocabulary lesson. In addition, fathers are also more likely to communicate with non-verbal cues, grunts, and

facial expressions. Girls and boys who grow up learning from their fathers will be better able to communicate with other males as they enter school and the work world.

Not every man needs to be a stereotypical alpha male in order to be a good dad. Nor do mothers need to be the model of June Cleaver. As I explain in my book *Secure Daughters, Confident Sons: How Parents Guide Their Children into Authentic Masculinity and Femininity*, there are a hundred different ways to be a good man and a good woman. Compare Payton Manning and Yo-Yo Ma: two very different ways of being real men. Or contrast Margaret Thatcher and Jacqueline Kennedy: two very different ways of being undeniably female.

There is indeed a universal male nature, just as there is a female nature. If the Western world's effort to de-gender our children has taught us anything, it's that gender difference is far more than just a social construct.

The reality of distinct male and female natures extends far beyond the bedroom and bathroom. It shows itself on the playground, in the community, at the school, and on the street. Both a man and a woman are required for the creation of a new child, and both are equally indispensable for rearing that child. This holds true no matter what continent we live in, or in what century. To deny it is delusional. By building families and a culture that affirm the importance of both fathers and mothers, we can give our children – all of them – the childhood which they are entitled to, which they deserve, and which they require.

From WikiArt (public domain)

Jesus' Surprising Family Values

CHARLES E. MOORE

Above, detail from Vincent van Gogh's *Still Life: Potatoes in a Yellow Dish*

Jesus loved little children. According to the Gospel writers, he would place them front and center as an example of how to receive the good news, and he was indignant when his friends spoke sternly to them. He taught his followers that unless we become like children, we cannot enter the kingdom of God.

But Jesus does not appear to have the same admiration for the family. Here his teaching often seems harsh, even alarming. Jesus told a would-be disciple who wanted to show basic decency to his deceased father, "Let the dead bury their own dead" (Luke 9:60). He commanded his disciples: Leave parents, siblings, spouse – even "hate" them – and follow me. When his own mother and brothers came to see him, Jesus' reaction was terse: "Who are my mother and my brothers?" Looking at those seated around him he said, "Here are my mother and my brothers! Whoever does the will of God is my brother and sister and mother" (Mark 3:31–35).

Jesus himself founded no family – he took no wife, fathered no children, and even called some to be "eunuchs" (Matt. 19: 11–12). Contrary to the tradition that salvation is guaranteed by ancestry or that one's highest social obligation is to family, he reminded his listeners that the covenant that first drew God's people together was based not on bloodlines but on faith and the miraculous power of God (John 8:31–59).

This is why Jesus dethroned the biological family. While he never denied the family's worth as a creation of God, he made clear that its importance is not absolute; it is not the primary means by which God's grace is transmitted to this broken world. Something else is.

Jesus calls his disciples to give their allegiance first and foremost to him. Those who forsake human security, including their families, will receive "a hundredfold now in this age – houses, brothers and sisters, mothers and children, and fields, with persecutions – and in the age to come eternal life" (Mark 10:29–31). In calling into question the primacy of the family,

Jesus asks us to imagine a different social order, an all-encompassing community based not on natural ties but on discipleship. Jesus came to establish the new family of God, a family of disciples who follow him with the entirety of their lives (Matt. 10:34–37).

Rodney Clapp, in his book *Families at the Crossroads* (Intervarsity, 1993), notes how Jesus stretches the family beyond its natural state because his new social order transcends the old boundaries in which people love only their own. In Clapp's words, "It is through a new family, born again of the Spirit, that God's kingdom breaks into our world."

Jesus exalts children because they – not the powerful and the successful – teach us how to become part of this new family. While the disciples argue over who will be the greatest in the kingdom, Jesus places a small child before them as an answer (Mark 9:34–37). Children are dependent and relatively powerless; they teach us to become small so that God's kingdom may become great. When this happens, a new set of relationships is born of his Spirit under his cross. It is the church, God's first family, a life of shared sacrifice and community in which family ties are loosed for God to weave together, from many different strands, a new fabric. Only when we become like children and recognize our utter dependence upon God, and only when we put our natural families second, can this kind of society – the church – exist.

In Jesus' new family, things are turned upside down: the first are last, and the least are the greatest. Things aren't "natural." People are more valued than possessions, and love for our biological kindred gives way to serving everyone around us, even those most unlike us. Like children who pay little attention to race or social status, we enter a radically new way of relating to one another.

Paradoxically, within this new and greater family the natural family of parents and children is honored and can even be strengthened. When the first Christians spread the good news across the Mediterranean world, their witness contrasted sharply with the promiscuity and decadence of Roman society. Widows and orphans were cared for, and no one was in need, for entire congregations shared everything they had. Husbands learned self-discipline and self-sacrifice, and women were honored as co-equal heirs of salvation. The result was that the natural family was restored to what God originally intended.

Today there are countless problems undermining families, from divorce and poverty to pornography and drugs. But these problems are only symptoms of what ails us: the absence of community centered on God. The hyper-individualistic worldview that is the hallmark of our age is a threat to the family and to children far more insidious than underfunded schools or immoral lifestyles. This false creed tries to shove God out of the public realm and confine him to private spirituality. It promises that maximizing personal autonomy will bring happiness. Now that the infection runs so deep, it's no wonder that many families are in trouble.

Jesus calls us to pursue not only the good of those nearest and dearest to us, but to seek first the kingdom of God and his justice. He adds: "And then all these things will be given to you as well" (Matt. 6:33). We must put Christ and his church first. Only then will our marriages and our families be able to withstand the forces that threaten them. And more importantly, only then will we be able to advance the gospel of the kingdom in this fragmented world.

Charles E. Moore is the editor of Everyone Belongs to God: Discovering the Hidden Christ, *a collection of Christoph Friedrich Blumhardt's writings on mission to be published by Plough in spring 2015.*

Letter from the Texas-Mexico Border

Giving the Gift of Good Memories

KERSTIN KEIDERLING

"We tried to sleep in the desert but we couldn't because there were too many animals. They came right up to me and they had big eyes and I could see that they were lions." Lia and Cynthia, both nine-year-olds from El Salvador, stare at me from across the table, wide-eyed as they remember the night they spent with their mothers hiding from US Border Patrol. "There were many noises. I could tell that most of the animals were lions because of the noise they were making." Lia can't get that night out of her mind, but Cynthia comes to the rescue: "We once went to the zoo in the city. I saw many lions there." I latch on to that. "Really? What else did you see there?" Thankfully that's all it takes. They're off, talking about happier times when they didn't have to worry about gangs coming into their school, forcing them to hand over their lunch money and threatening that their mothers would be murdered if they told anyone.

Nor were these empty threats. Earlier this week I sat mute as a six-year-old described how a man in her village was killed with a machete, demonstrating the slash marks from her forehead to her chin on both sides of her face. He was left to die on the street near the school so when school let out the children had to pass him.

These girls are among thousands of families and unaccompanied minors who have made their way from their homes, mostly in El Salvador, Honduras, and Guatemala, to this country in search of safety. At first I wondered if the situations they are going into – crowded living conditions, minimum wage jobs, city schools in a foreign language – are any better than what they're leaving. But after hearing just a few of their stories I realized the depth of the horror they're fleeing.

As the numbers of immigrants streaming into the United States grew in the beginning of June, Catholic Charities in McAllen, Texas, decided to do something for the hundreds of families they saw dropped off by Border Patrol at the local bus station. They opened an assistance center three blocks from the bus station with tables loaded with donated clothing. They set up showers and, together with the Salvation Army, provided food. Because many of the arriving parents had had little or no sleep for days, the city of McAllen donated tents so families could sleep.

The local organizers welcome volunteers from all over the country who come to help out. Coordinating the resources of multiple charities with waves of volunteers coming for short stints is a tough assignment, but the teamwork I've seen here over the last few months is impressive. Families have driven from as far away as Pennsylvania with a truck full of donations, ready to do anything to help, even to look foolish with their halting attempts at Spanish. Churches have come on mission trips and the Salvation Army rotates teams once a week. Everyone comes with the goal of welcoming these families into our country, and the enthusiasm is infectious.

Save the Children's "Child Friendly Space" in McAllen, Texas

Courtesy of Save the Children

Courtesy of Save the Children

Language seems to be hardly a barrier here; somehow the message gets through.

This past summer, after reading countless articles on the border crisis and watching footage of mothers and children clinging to trains and buses, risking their lives to enter the United States, my church wanted to do something to respond. My friend Amy and I volunteered with Save the Children, a nonprofit organization that goes into disaster zones all over the world to help families and children recover. Their signature child protection program, Child Friendly Spaces, allows children who have experienced a traumatic event to play and be kids again. Here in McAllen, Save the Children has set up a Child Friendly Space in the corner of the Sacred Heart recreation center where children can play while they wait for the buses that will take them to relatives farther north.

I spend my days looking after the children who come to play. Some days there's only one child, some days there are fifty. Some stay the whole day, others for only half an hour. Each child brings a story, and their stories are often also the stories of their parents and grandparents. One afternoon a nine-year-old with whom I was making bracelets told me that she and her father were going to Houston to meet her mother. I asked her when she had last seen her mother. Nine years ago, she told me. She'd lived with her grandmother her whole life. I asked if she was excited. She wasn't sure. As I hugged her goodbye later that day, I could only wish her good luck and pray that this country would be kind to her.

I never tire of seeing the children come into our space. At first they are wary. They have come straight from Border Patrol, and we may be the first smiling faces they have seen for days. But when they see the toys and other children having a good time, they start to forget themselves. Soon they are right in there with the rest, racing cars or coloring pictures of princesses. Best of all, when the mothers see their children relaxed and smiling, they start smiling too.

I have been here for several months. The constant stream of new faces, child after child, keeps me stretched between heartbreak and inspiration. Shortly before coming here, I read a quote from Dostoyevsky: "You must know that there is nothing higher and stronger and more wholesome and good for life in the future than some good memory, especially a memory of childhood. . . . For if a man has only one good memory left in his heart, even that may keep him from evil. . . . And if he carries many such memories with him into life, he is safe for the end of his days." These words guide me as I try to give these children some good memories to take with them as they go out from our Child Friendly Space into an uncertain future.

Kerstin Keiderling has worked in McAllen, Texas since July 2014 with Save the Children, an international humanitarian organization promoting the welfare of children. www.savethechildren.org

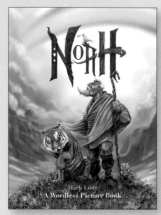

Noah
A Wordless Picture Book
Mark Ludy

Plough, 2014 (64 pages, hardcover, 8.5 x 11)
www.plough.com

A hundred years before the Great Flood, a man named Noah came home talking crazy.

God wanted him to build the biggest ship the world had ever seen. The future of humanity depended on it. How would his wife respond? What would the neighbors think? Was it even feasible?

Ludy's new book is a playful reimagining of one of the greatest stories of all time, to be enjoyed by children and adults alike. The pictures take their cues from Genesis, chapters 6 to 9, which can be read while viewing the pictures. Selected excerpts appear in the following pages.

Mark Ludy has written or illustrated eight children's books including *The Farmer, The Flower Man, The Grump,* and *Jujo the Youngest Tribesman.* When he's not immersed in his sketchbooks, you'll find him in schools promoting art and literacy. He lives in Colorado with his wife, daughter, and two sons.

Noah

A Wordless Story

MARK LUDY

Continued in the book. . .

Featured Books from Plough

Easter Stories: Classic Tales for the Holy Season

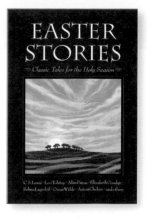

Edited by Miriam LeBlanc. Everyone who believes Easter is about more than bunnies and eggs will be grateful for this new collection of short stories that shed light on the deeper meaning of the season. Selected for their spiritual value and literary integrity, these twenty-six tales evoke the spirit of Easter in a way that will captivate readers young and old. Includes time-honored favorites from world-renowned storytellers such as C. S. Lewis, Leo Tolstoy, Selma Lagerlöf, Alan Paton, Oscar Wilde, Elizabeth Goudge, Maxim Gorky, Ruth Sawyer, Anton Chekhov, and Walter Wangerin – as well as many you've never heard before.

Don't miss our companion volume, *Home for Christmas: Stories for Young and Old.*

Bread and Wine: Readings for Lent and Easter

Anthology. A time for soul-searching and spiritual preparation, Lent is traditionally observed by daily reading and reflection. Culled from the wealth of twenty centuries, the seventy-two selections in *Bread and Wine* cover the breadth and depth of Christian writers: Augustine, Thomas à Kempis, John Donne, Frederick Buechner, Oswald Chambers, G. K. Chesterton, Blaise Pascal, Dorothy Sayers, Jane Kenyon, Wendell Berry, Thomas Merton, Henri Nouwen, Oscar Romero, Christina Rossetti, Edith Stein, Walter Wangerin, William Willimon, Dorothy Day, Brennan Manning, Philip Yancey, and many more. A companion to *Watch for the Light: Readings for Advent and Christmas.*

> "Has there ever been a more hard-hitting, beautifully written, theologically inclusive anthology of writings for Lent and Easter? It's doubtful . . . . *Caveat lector:* no one should have this much pleasure during Lent!"   —*Publishers Weekly* (starred review)

Rasmus and the Vagabond

By Astrid Lindgren. Readers have told us how hard it is to find quality, family-friendly children's fiction of the sort they grew up on. We've listened. In this first installment, we revive a long-out-of-print classic from one of the most beloved children's authors of all time, Astrid Lindgren, the creator of Pippi Longstocking. After running away from an orphanage, nine-year-old Rasmus finds the world a cold and unfriendly place until he meets an extraordinary tramp called Paradise Oscar. Together they discover hidden treasure, dodge a shady pair of villains, and rescue a prisoner. A gripping plot interweaving cops and robbers, a deserted village, and a desperate chase leads to a surprising, thoroughly satisfying ending.

Provocations: Spiritual Writings of Kierkegaard

Edited by Charles E. Moore. Søren Kierkegaard, the philosopher known as the father of modern existentialism, is a famous figure. But who was Kierkegaard the Christian? This highly readable compilation of the best of Kierkegaard's spiritual thought contains a little of everything: his attacks on "the mediocre shell" of conventional Christianity, his brilliant parables, and his wise and witty sayings.

> "In a culture awash in religious silliness, Kierkegaard's bracing metaphors expose our mediocrities and energize us with a clarified sense of what it means to follow Jesus."
> —Eugene Peterson

> "One of the top ten books of the year. Readable and spiritually vibrant."
> —*Christianity Today*

www.plough.com

Free access to dozens of e-books for subscribers

Reclaiming a Literary Giant

Ernst Wiechert, the master novelist who survived Buchenwald

DANIEL HALLOCK

"It may happen that a nation ceases to distinguish between good and evil," warned Ernst Wiechert, a German novelist and professor, in a 1935 speech to his students, many of whom were already enthusiastic National Socialists. "It may then be that it will win a gladiator's glory . . . but the scales will already have been hung above this people." The text of Wiechert's talk, titled "Address to the German Youth," was baked into a loaf of bread and smuggled out of the country for publication by anti-Nazi refugees in Moscow.

At the time of Wiechert's speech, his country was slipping blindly into Hitler-worship. At first, although Wiechert refused to lend his popularity as a novelist to the Nazi cause, he kept his criticism veiled. "He is a sorcerer," complained an official in Joseph Goebbels' Ministry of Propaganda, "but he refuses to use his magic on our side." That changed two years later, however, when Wiechert heard news of the arrest of Martin Niemöller, the famous Lutheran pastor who resisted Nazi control of the German Protestant church. Incensed, he wrote an open letter criticizing the government and announcing his support of Niemöller and his family.

Daniel Hallock is the author of Six Months to Live: Learning from a Young Man with Cancer, *which will be reissued by Plough in spring 2015. He lives in Nonington, Kent, England.*

Wiechert paid for this bold act of defiance with four months in the Buchenwald concentration camp. On his release, Goebbels threatened to have him killed if he publicly protested again. Wiechert was blacklisted; no publisher would risk releasing a new book by him until after the war. The single exception was *Das einfache Leben* ("The Simple Life") in 1939, a celebration of life in nature with similarities to Thoreau's *Walden*. To Goebbels's fury, the censor's suppression order for this book failed to reach the publisher before it went to press, and in just three years it sold over a quarter million copies.

After the war, on November 11, 1945, Wiechert made another "Address to the German Youth," calling for national repentance and castigating those who sought to glorify German war heroes:

> The heroes and martyrs of these last years are not those returning with victor's laurels from countries we defeated. Rather, they are those who have died and suffered ruin behind prison bars and barbed wire, to Germany's honor. For this kind of honor was the only kind to be had.

Such words fell harshly on the ears of those post-war Germans who wished to forget the crimes in which they had been complicit. Wiechert increasingly lost his popularity among readers, and even fellow writers, many of them socialist, turned their backs on him, charging him with back-to-nature romanticism and "Old Prussian pietism" (in the words of Hungarian Marxist philosopher György Lukács). Frustrated, Wiechert left Germany for Switzerland in 1948, where he died two years later. Gradually his books went out of print in Germany (though not in Poland) and dropped out of the literary canon. A courageous voice was silenced again.

While a prisoner in Buchenwald, Wiechert was put to work as a stone carrier and later assigned to the camp's "surface drainage crew." As Alfred Werner later reported in an obituary in

Commentary, the once-celebrated author, then nearing fifty, became weak and tubercular, his hands and feet grossly swollen. He was shocked to the core by the horror he had witnessed. He "felt a crack run through God's image [man], a crack that would never heal."

If this healing never came to Wiechert personally, he dreamed of it. When he died in 1950, he left a startlingly honest novel that portrays what such redemption might look like. Published posthumously, *Tidings* is a novel of Dostoyevskian depth which portrays an inner journey. While spare in historical detail, it is populated with characters both victimized and complicit, all striving toward restoration.

First published as *Missa sine nomine* – "Mass without a name" – the novel is set in the Rhön Mountains of central Germany after the end of the Second World War. Baron Amadeus, the main character, is one of three brothers of German nobility who have been separated by the war. The novel opens with Amadeus on the road home from concentration camp, still wearing his striped camp uniform. He reaches the family castle to find it inhabited by American troops while his brothers live in a small shepherd's hut. Amadeus is reunited with his brothers, but is inwardly isolated by the suffering he has witnessed and experienced, and by his own guilt: although gentle by nature, he had shot and killed "the hangman" of the camp. He tells his brothers:

> I have killed . . . with this hand . . . and what is more . . . I would kill again at any time, if one of the faces which smiled while they tortured appeared here. There something within me changed; something that I had was taken away from me. . . . You have remained the same.

But no one is untouched by the war. The oldest brother, tormented by the memory of the night when he abandoned the peasant families in his charge to the onslaught of troops, seeks to make

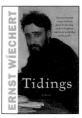

Tidings: A Novel
Ernst Wiechert
(Plough, hardcover, 305 pages)

John Singer Sargent, *Blue Gentians*

reparation by tending to the displaced persons who occupy the family castle. The second looks for healing in the land itself, by working the soil and allowing nature to cleanse his soul.

Scarred by the atrocities of the war, all the characters – and the natural world they inhabit – grow toward restoration. Only Amadeus, despite the compassionate ministrations of his brothers, seems unable even to make an attempt at finding peace.

Then peace pursues him in the form of a young woman who – stripped of conscience by the brutal philosophies that she was raised with and pregnant with the child of a fugitive Nazi official – attempts to kill him. After the attempt she loses her mind, and Amadeus finds himself compelled, by a remaining spark of decency, to protect her as she awaits the birth of her child. Amadeus is led slowly toward love and sacrifice, and toward the God who was born as a helpless child in a manger, consoled and challenged by a cast of fellow sufferers.

Jakob, an old Jewish salesman whose family perished in the fires of the Holocaust, counsels Amadeus:

If an old man is allowed to speak . . . he would kindly beg the gentleman to let the Lord our God live in his face. . . . The Holy One, blessed be He . . . is wandering and looks for a place where He can rest. He looks into the faces of men and goes past. The face of Herr Baron is not yet a place where He can rest. The face of

Herr Baron is still occupied by the dead and by himself. You must put aside all that belongs to yourself.

A parson named Wittkopp, who has also lost wife and child to the war, speaks to Amadeus of the privilege of caring for the shattered young woman:

You are the only one . . . on whom such an obligation could be laid. . . . You must not do it out of generosity. You must realize how much you owe to the poor girl for the opportunity to perfect yourself. Without her it might have been impossible for you.

Tidings closes with an otherworldly peace, as Amadeus allows himself to imagine a world in which the innocent spirit of little children might thrive once more:

All the anguish of the dark hours behind the barbed wire . . . where he had been at the gates of hell; where not only suffering, horror and death had revealed themselves, but what was more – where man had revealed himself. He who had overcome this . . . who had not lost the image of man and the image of God with it forever – he could now well stand still, when the girl's cheek rested on his shoulder . . . He could slowly enlarge the small circle of life, without an effort because it was his lot – his lot that the children from the castle now came more and more frequently to his hut, and that he could bring a little gladness into their needy lives. . . . All the wonderful things, little things which had lit up the world of his own childhood, and which had been forgotten in a time when only searchlights and great conflagrations had lit up the dark scene, and for which no one outside the shepherd's hut had time. . . .

The novel's pages are imbued with poetic beauty and intensity, exploring the mystical work of God in the heart and soul in the aftermath of unimaginable suffering. It is the condensed wisdom of Wiechert's own personal anguish and hard-won faith, like gold refined in the fire. ✒

Kingdom Conspiracy: Returning to the Radical Mission of the Local Church
Scot McKnight (Brazos Press)

"Kingdom" is the most misused, misunderstood word in the Christian lexicon, McKnight argues. On one hand are those who use it as shorthand for social justice, "good deeds done by good people in the public sector for the common good." On the other side are those who have relegated it to purely religious "moments of redemption." But the kingdom of God, McKnight reminds us, is inseparable from the reign of Jesus in his Body, the church—a united people of God through whom he can work in the world.

A Farewell to Mars: An Evangelical Pastor's Journey toward the Biblical Gospel of Peace
Brian Zahnd (David C Cook)

This may be a personal journey, but Zahnd's bold and incisive message is anything but private. Individual salvation, Zahnd realizes, cannot be divorced from Jesus' clear teachings about violence and power, vengeance and peacemaking, which have decidedly political and social implications. From a surprising corner comes a fresh, accessible introduction to what the Bible actually has to say about the way of Jesus, the Prince of Peace.

A Child Shall Lead Them: Martin Luther King Jr., Young People, and the Movement
Rufus Burrow Jr. (Fortress Press)

This well-researched book tells the story of the young people who helped define the Civil Rights Movement. Burrow shows how much King respected their youthful vision and passion, sometimes steering them, but often following their more daring lead. Burrow dreams of inspiring a younger generation to change their world; it will take more than a history book to do that, but still, he's contributed an enduring testimony to the power of youth.

Loving Samuel: Suffering, Dependence, and the Calling of Love
Aaron D. Cobb (Wipf and Stock)

Grief can open our hearts to God like nothing else. Months before their son Samuel's birth, Cobb and his wife Alisha learned that he had Trisomy 18, a chromosomal abnormality "incompatible with life." They welcomed him as a gift from God anyway, and held him for five precious hours. Not a word is wasted in this slim, luminous collection of a father's reflections while waiting and preparing for his son's birth and death ("an unimaginably long, short stretch of time") and during the season of grief that would follow.

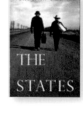

The Disunited States
Vladimir Pozner (Seven Stories)

Translated into English for the first time, this outsider's lyrical and perceptive portrait of America in the 1930s is an unearthed treasure. Pozner, a French novelist and screenwriter, captures the essence of a nation of contradictions at a moment of economic and spiritual crisis uncannily reminiscent of our times. Much of the book – including the extraordinary tour-de-force that is the first chapter – is drawn from local newspaper accounts. At times, the distance between our lives and those Pozner describes seems to dissolve, and we're suddenly face to face with real human beings whose hopes and heartbreaks are strangely close to us. ⬎

The Editors

Does ISIS Prove Nonviolence Wrong?

MAKING PEACE WITH JUST WARRIORS

An Interview with Ron Sider

A young boy at the funeral of a fighter from the Women's Protection Unit, a militia made up of Kurdish women. The fallen fighter was killed in action defending the besieged Syrian border town of Kobani in November 2014.

Leading Christians have lent moral backing to military action against the self-proclaimed "Islamic State" (ISIS), citing the Just War doctrine. Christian pacifists, meanwhile, have struggled to suggest convincing alternatives at a time when preaching nonviolence can seem naïve, even heartless. But does the Just War tradition give its adherents a blank check in such a situation? We turned to Ron Sider, founder of Evangelicals for Social Action and a dean among Christian pacifists, who lately has been talking about a truce with Just War Christians – while challenging all of us to go beyond easy answers.

Plough: *In your forthcoming book* Nonviolent Action: What Christian Ethics Demands but Most Christians Have Never Really Tried *(Baker, 2015), you argue that both Just War Christians and pacifists have an obligation to confront injustice with nonviolent resistance. Can you elaborate?*

Ron Sider: Nonviolent action is an ethical demand that applies to both pacifists and Just War Christians. All Christians are called to be peacemakers. But neither pacifists nor Just War adherents have made much careful, systematically planned use of nonviolent action, even though again and again nonviolent action has proved to be effective. So that's the core of my message. Nonviolent action, if given a chance, is stunningly successful. For example, the Solidarity movement defied the Soviet Union and they won.

Over the past half year, ISIS forces in Iraq and Syria have committed horrific atrocities. Most people, including many churches, believe that nonviolent methods won't work. Do you agree?

People committed to nonviolence do not always have instant solutions to the messes that military policies get us into. There is plenty of evidence that shows how in different kinds of situations nonviolent strategies have been amazingly effective. But in the short run, nonviolent actions are not always, or automatically, successful. It's not very likely, at least at this point, that ISIS will respond to a nonviolent peacemaking team, or even to substantial numbers of nonviolent people taking action.

Of course, military action isn't always automatically successful either, and often has unintended consequences. ISIS terrorism, according to some, has only been able to flourish because of the decisions made by the United States and its allies in 2001 and 2003 to go to war in Afghanistan and Iraq. What's your view?

ISIS has certainly not come out of a vacuum. In 2003, except for some American evangelical leaders, the global Christian community said that even on the basis of Just War criteria, invading Iraq was not justified. The Pope said it. Christian leaders around the world said it. Many American Christian leaders said it. So I think one thing peacemakers, including pacifists like myself, need to do is to help their societies actually apply the Just War criteria carefully and consistently. That doesn't mean presidents won't ignore us, but if enough people speak out and enough political pressure builds, it can make a difference.

Yet even apart from ISIS, the idea of nonviolent action strikes most people as unrealistic, somewhat like the medieval Children's Crusade.

This is why we must re-educate people. We now know that nonviolence works. It has worked again and again, as we have seen especially in the last fifty years. And it has worked even without very much training or very much analysis. I don't pretend to be a sophisticated tactician of nonviolent campaigns, but I tell story after story in my book about amazingly successful nonviolent campaigns.

For example?

We can go back to the first-century Jews who offered to die rather than allow Roman military standards to be displayed in Jerusalem, causing Pontius Pilate to remove the standards. In the fifth century, Pope Leo I rode to meet Attila the Hun and his armies as they approached

THE CRITERIA: WHAT'S A "JUST WAR"?

Just War doctrine is accepted by a wide range of Christian traditions. As summarized in the Catholic *Catechism,* it requires that the following "strict conditions" must be fulfilled for a war to be legitimate:

- The damage inflicted by the aggressor on the nation or community of nations must be lasting, grave, and certain;
- All other means of putting an end to it must have been shown to be impractical or ineffective;

- There must be serious prospects of success;
- The use of arms must not produce evils or disorders graver than the evil to be eliminated. The power of modern means of destruction weighs very heavily in evaluating this condition. (*CCC*, para. 2309)

In addition, Just War doctrine requires that war be conducted according to moral law, with humane treatment of non combatants, prisoners, and the

wounded. Acts of extermination or mass destruction are prohibited.

Although Just War doctrine goes back at least as far as Augustine of Hippo (AD 354–430), it was not the teaching of the early church. In fact, Christian leaders of the first centuries overwhelmingly prohibited the use of lethal force for any reason. See Ron Sider, *The Early Church on Killing: A Comprehensive Sourcebook on War, Abortion, and Capital Punishment* (Baker Academic, 2012).

Pacifists
must be
willing
to run
the same
risks in a
nonviolent
struggle as
soldiers do
in battle.

Rome and turned them back. Then there's the nineteenth-century truce between Argentina and Chile that was effected by a bishop from each side who preceded the troops. The twentieth century was rich with examples, the best known of course being Gandhi's leadership in India and Martin Luther King Jr.'s peaceful Civil Rights Movement in this country. But there are countless others from across the globe: peaceful demonstrations in El Salvador and Guatemala that contributed to the collapse of violent dictatorships; a "nonviolent fleet" consisting of three kayaks, three canoes, and a rubber raft that blocked the path of a huge freighter and helped stop the flow of arms between the United States and Pakistan; the Alagamar land struggle in Brazil in the late 1970s; and the list goes on. Christian Peacemaker Teams have had real success in reducing violence in Colombia.

In addition, there are historical might-have-beens, such as in the early 1990s at the time of the collapse of Yugoslavia, which led to war in the Balkans. Nonviolent action would have had a powerful effect if at that time leaders from the Orthodox, Catholic, and Protestant churches had marched into the region of conflict and said: "We come here in the name of Jesus. You can kill us if you want to, but we're going to stand between you and your religious and ethnic enemies."

Similarly, I believe nonviolent direct action might have worked in confronting Robert Mugabe in Zimbabwe.

Okay, but are there no exceptions?

My intent is not to convince people that nonviolence always works quickly or easily; I'm not going to argue that in every situation of violence there is a short-term nonviolent solution. Rather, my argument is this: Look at all the historical successes of nonviolent action, despite the fact that we haven't invested much of anything in terms of time, money, study, and strategizing. With that in mind, what we need to do across the board in the Christian church, whether you are a pacifist or a Just War person,

is to call for a lot more investment in nonviolent action. We need something comparable to the war colleges – academies where we can carefully analyze nonviolent tactics and determine what works and what doesn't. Compared to what we have for military training, for nonviolent action we have almost nothing.

I think that Christian Peacemaker Teams and other such interventions are one way to do that; they ought to be vastly expanded. But it's also important to keep in mind the broader context, as Glen Stassen points out in the book *Just Peacemaking.* He and many other scholars – some of them pacifist and some of them not – have shown that there is a wide range of nonviolent ways that can help resolve conflict in the world. I think an honest, realistic, sophisticated analysis of how, when, and why nonviolent tactics work will help us understand more clearly where it's wise to invest time and to engage.

You've said that nonviolent action is a mandate of Christian ethics whether one believes in Just War doctrine or in pacifism. In fact, your book carries a foreword by Richard Mouw, the former president of Fuller Theological Seminary, who calls himself a "defender of Just War theory." How might Just War adherents and pacifists work together?

Pacifists and Just War Christians need to assess each situation together. With some frequency, there will be situations where applying the Just War criteria will lead us to conclude, "This war should not be fought, this invasion should not take place. An alternative must be found." There may be, however, other situations where Just War Christians will conclude that they must go to war.

But the Just War theory requires that war is a last resort, and until you've tried all reasonable nonviolent alternatives, war is not a last resort. Unless Just War Christians are ready to test all reasonable nonviolent alternatives, the Just War position has no integrity. Likewise, pacifists have no moral right to pretend their way is better unless they are willing to run the same risks in a nonviolent struggle against evil as soldiers do in battle.

You've been at this work for decades, calling on Christians to live justly and to take responsibility for peacemaking. Do you see signs of progress?

It's been thirty-seven years since my book *Rich Christians in an Age of Hunger* was published – I'm just revising it for the sixth edition, which will come out next year. At the time I wrote it, most evangelical leaders said that the primary mission of the church is saving souls and doing evangelism. There was a huge debate for several decades over whether or not social action and working for social justice was also an important part of the mission of the church. That debate has been won almost across the board. Evangelical leaders now advocate that we're supposed to do evangelism and we're supposed to do social justice. By contrast, in theologically liberal and mainline circles such a holistic approach hasn't been so readily embraced. If you don't believe in the deity of Christ – if you don't believe that Jesus is the only way to salvation – then there's not much point in proclaiming the gospel. But among most evangelicals around the world today, evangelism and social action are an integral whole.

Take for example the International Justice Mission and the way it has grown so fast, or think of the Justice Conference and of all the younger evangelicals who are involved in it. And as a matter of fact, over the last four decades poverty has been substantially reduced in the world. Of course, there are still around 1.2 billion people who try to live on $1.25 a day. There is still desperate poverty in the world, yet the progress has been enormous.

In Christian circles nowadays, it sometimes seems that "justice" has become an overused word. Are we in danger of losing sight of the power of the gospel and how it can change people's lives?

I'm actually quite worried about this. I want to say: "Hey, do you care as much about

Jordi Bernabeu Farrús / Wikimedia Commons

evangelism as you do about social justice? Do you care as much about how there are millions of people who have never heard about Jesus as you do about the fact that there's enormous poverty and injustice in the world?" I certainly do not want to go back to a one-sided emphasis on evangelism, but neither do I want to see a repeat of a one-sided social gospel movement whose only concern is to improve the outer conditions of the world.

You've recommended that the church should make a massive investment into nonviolent action by researching tactics and building institutions to carry it out. How would you respond to those who say, "Hold on – is that really the church's task?"

As I've said for decades now, the first thing the church should do is be the church. If it's not being the church – whether it's crossing racial lines or working for justice for the poor – then preaching policy changes to the government is nothing but hypocrisy. It's a farce to try to persuade Washington to do what we Christians don't live out. Our first priority is to be the church and to live out the justice and peace of Christ.

But as we do this, we will also be compelled to reach out to others, and in so doing we will not only tell people about Jesus, how to follow him and accept him as the Lord and Savior he is, but in his name and motivated by his love we will work to change society. Christ called us to be peacemakers and to spread the gospel of peace in every way we can. That is where we need to put our energies and resources.

Interview by Peter Mommsen on October 9, 2014.

A Kurdish refugee in Mursitpinar, Turkey, who fled the fighting around Kobani in October 2014

Photograph by Harry Mattison

Blood and Ink

The Making of El Salvador's Company of Martyrs

ROBERT LASALLE-KLEIN

Mourners during the funeral for Archbishop Romero, San Salvador, March 30, 1980

Twenty-five years ago, on November 16, 1989, six Jesuit priests and two women were murdered by US-trained Salvadoran special forces on the campus of the University of Central America in San Salvador.

The killings sent shock waves through the United States Congress, which was monitoring human rights in El Salvador. For the past decade, Congress had been funding the right-wing Salvadoran government's civil war against rebels demanding political and economic reform. However, these appropriations depended on official certifications by the Reagan and Bush administrations that

human-rights abuses by El Salvador's government and paramilitary forces were declining.

Yet shortly after 10 p.m. on November 15, Colonel René Emilio Ponce, chief of staff of the Armed Forces of El Salvador, in collusion with the country's highest ranking military officials, ordered Colonel Guillermo Alfredo Benavides to eliminate the Jesuits at the university, specifically Ignacio Ellacuría, the university president

Robert Lasalle-Klein, professor of religious studies and philosophy at Holy Names University and cofounder of the Oakland Catholic Worker, is the author of Blood and Ink: Ignacio Ellacuría, Jon Sobrino, and the Jesuit Martyrs *of the University of Central America (Orbis, 2014); this article is adapted from the book.*

and the country's leading public intellectual: "Kill Father Ellacuría and leave no witnesses."[1] The meeting took place at the national military academy, of which Colonel Benavides was director. Within the hour, he summoned Lieutenant Ricardo Espinoza, a young graduate of San Salvador's Jesuit high school, and ordered him to carry out the assassination. The targets included not only Ellacuría but also Lieutenant Espinoza's former high-school principal. "It's them or us!" Benavides told Espinoza.[2] The young officer, who attempted to hide his identity with camouflage grease, later testified that his eyes filled with tears as he hurriedly left the scene of the crime after giving the order for the killing.[3]

The United Nations Commission on the Truth for El Salvador states that around 2:30 a.m. on November 16, Ellacuría and four fellow Spanish-born Jesuits were executed with machine guns by Espinoza's unit as they lay face down in the grass behind the Jesuit residence at the university. One neighbor reports that "just before the gunfire" she heard "rhythmic whispering, like a psalmody of a group in prayer."[4] Minutes later, Elba Ramos, a cook for the university, and her sixteen-year-old daughter Celina were repeatedly shot as they huddled in each other's arms in the Jesuit residence, where they had sought refuge. The brutality ended with the murder of an elderly Salvadoran-born Jesuit priest in his room. Several sources later testified that El Salvador's newly elected president, Alfredo Cristiani, was present at the national military academy at the time when the attack was planned and that he met with Colonel Ponce and other military officials during the operation.

In addition to Father Ellacuría, the Jesuits who died included Father Ignacio Martín-Baró, a university vice president and the director of El Salvador's only functioning public-opinion poll; Father Segundo Montes, director of the university's Human Rights Institute and superior of the Jesuit community; Father Amando López, professor of theology and philosophy and former president of the university's sister institution in Managua; Father Joaquin López y López, national director of Fe y Alegría, a program for children in poverty; and Father Juan Ramón Moreno, assistant director of the newly constructed Óscar Romero Pastoral Center, built by the Jesuits to commemorate the archbishop of San Salvador who had died nine years earlier by a rightwing assassin's bullet.

Why Were They Killed?

One month after the murders, Major Eric Warren Buckland, a senior US military advisor in El Salvador, testified that his Salvadoran counterpart, Colonel Carlos Armando Avilés Buitrago, chief of psychological operations for the Salvadoran Joint Command, informed him in advance of the planned killing; afterward the same source confirmed both that the crime had been committed by specific high-ranking Salvadoran military officers, and that it was being covered up.[5] Major Buckland's account matched the testimony of Lucía Cerna, a neighbor of the Jesuit fathers and the only living witness to the crime. Both Major Buckland and Cerna would come under intense pressure from the FBI to back away from their stories implicating Salvadoran forces; Buckland soon recanted his admission of prior knowledge of the killings. *Newsweek* later reported, "The [George H. W. Bush] administration didn't want that story to come out . . . because it wasn't productive to the conduct of the war."[6]

1 United Nations, *Report of the Commission on the Truth for El Salvador: From Madness to Hope: The Twelve-Year War in El Salvador* (March 15, 1993), 50.

2 Extrajudicial statements of Lt. José Ricardo Espinoza Guerra and Lt. Yusshy René Mendoza Vallecillos, cited in Martha Doggett, *Death Foretold: The Jesuit Murders in El Salvador* (Georgetown University Press, Lawyers Committee for Human Rights, 1993), 65.

3 Extrajudicial confession of Lt. José Ricardo Espinoza Guerra, cited from "Narración de los hechos," prepared by the Jesuits of Central America, which appeared in *Estudios centroamericanos (ECA)* nos. 493–494 (November–December 1989): 1162.

4 Doggett, *Death Foretold*, 282, 68.

5 Sworn statement by Eric Warren Buckland, January 11, 1990, handwritten addendum, Washington, DC, p. 10 (on file at Lawyers Committee for Human Rights). Cited in Doggett, *Death Foretold*, 225.

6 Doggett, *Death Foretold*, 228.

Thus the orders to kill Father Ellacuría and his colleagues came from the highest levels of the Salvadoran military and may have been approved by the country's president, possibly with the knowledge of US military officials. For the Salvadoran government, the killings were extraordinarily risky; if they came to light they would implicate the entire military command structure and embarrass the United States.

Why take such a high-stakes gamble in order to kill one priest and a handful of associates? Evidently, the Salvadoran government viewed Ignacio Ellacuría and the University of Central America (UCA) as a serious threat to the United States' continued backing. The government was well aware that if the US Congress became concerned about human-rights abuses by its Salvadoran ally, it might withdraw its crucial support. Inconveniently, Ellacuría and his fellow Jesuits at the UCA were scrupulously documenting the government's systemic violations of human rights and its vicious repression of Salvadoran civil society. What's more, they publicly advocated peace negotiations with the rebels in order to put an end to the cycle of violence. To the country's governing elites, Ellacuría and his colleagues were jeopardizing the US support they needed to win a definitive victory over a leftist insurgency. They were traitors, and deserved to be treated as such.

The UCA Jesuits, by contrast, believed that it was their duty as Christians and Catholics to speak up for human rights and to advocate for a negotiated peace. Their vision was grounded in the teaching of the "preferential option for the poor" issued by the 1968 conference of Latin American bishops meeting in Medellín, Colombia, in response to the recently concluded Vatican II council. This "preferential option," they believed, required Christians to share God's special love for the poor and downtrodden as

illustrated throughout the Old and New Testaments. Echoing the language of Medellín, the university's 1979 mission statement declares that "the most explicit testimony of the Christian inspiration of the UCA will be putting itself really at the service of the people in such a way that in this service it allows itself to be oriented by the oppressed people themselves."[7]

There was an influence on the Jesuits' work more immediate than Medellín's teaching of social justice: the example of the martyr Archbishop Óscar Romero. Ellacuría would speak of the UCA Jesuits' "commitment to do in our university way what [Archbishop Romero] did in his pastoral way."[8] His colleague Jon Sobrino, a UCA Jesuit who survived the 1989 killings because he happened to be away from campus that night, argues that Ellacuría and the UCA learned to fulfill their mission by watching Romero run the San Salvador archdiocese from the perspective of a preferential option for the poor.

Thus the Jesuits of the UCA and Óscar Romero formed a company of martyrs bound together by a common conviction that the gospel must become good news to the poor. No outcome could have seemed less likely to anyone who knew of the active antagonism with which Romero's and Ellacuría's relationship began. Their remarkable story is told in the following pages, starting at the beginning.

Óscar Romero, Guardian of Orthodoxy 1970–1974

The Central American Jesuits began reorganizing their work in the early 1970s in an effort to embrace the Medellín call to stand with the poor. They understood this to mean actively supporting the rights of campesinos and civilian movements promoting social, economic, and political reform and the end of military rule. Ellacuría and the UCA worked

7 "Las funciones fundamentales de la universidad y su operativización," *Planteamiento universitario 1989* (UCA Editores, 1989), 47.
8 Ignacio Ellacuría, "La UCA ante el doctorado concedido a Monseñor Romero," *Escritos teológicos,* III (UCA Editores, 2002), 102; reprinted from *ECA* no. 437 (1985): 168.

Children mingle with insurgents in rebel-held territory in El Salvador, 1988.

throughout the decade to reframe the university's "principal mission as that of being the critical and creative conscience"[9] of the country and by taking positions in favor of urgent reforms to address the marginalization of the country's impoverished majorities.

Óscar Romero emerged at the same moment as one of the Jesuit's chief opponents among the Salvadoran bishops. He was then an auxiliary bishop in the San Salvador archdiocese and secretary of the bishops' conference of El Salvador. Romero's actions and statements from 1970 to 1976 betray a deep suspicion and even hostility toward Ellacuría's interpretation of Medellín as a call for the church to become more involved in movements for social change.

Reacting to the ferment following Vatican II, Romero was tradionalist in his approach to the role of the church in society. His approach has been called "quasi-corporatist," and it finds support in certain statements in the documents of Medellín, side by side with affirmations of the preferential option for the poor.[10] According to this view, the church's role is that of a unifying social institution, promoting what Medellín calls "socialization understood as a sociocultural process of personalization and communal growth" so that "all of the sectors of society, . . . [especially] the social-economic sphere, should, because of justice and brotherhood, transcend antagonisms in order to become agents of national and continental development."[11]

Romero's commitment to this vision of the church as unifier and social glue, along with other more personal factors, rendered him deeply suspicious of theological and pastoral approaches involving prophetic denunciations of state-sponsored violence. Romero's public statements and writings from this period as editor of the diocesan newspaper *Orientación* consistently characterize such views as politically naive distortions of Catholic teaching; such approaches, he suggested, were unduly influenced by communist ideas, and dangerously politicized the role of the church in Salvadoran society.

In the tinderbox atmosphere of El Salvador, Romero's accusations had real consequences. His very public attacks against clergy who were critical of the government helped to marginalize their voices and provided cover for repressive actions against those calling for change. In early 1972, for example, the Central Elections Council, which was known to be controlled by a pro-military faction, fraudulently declared Colonel Arturo Armando Molina winner of that year's presidential election. Molina's opponents had run on a platform promising desperately needed agrarian reforms. When the stolen election was exposed by a UCA investigation, many seminarians refused to sing at the liturgy for Molina's inauguration. They charged that the church, by allowing this event to be celebrated in the cathedral in the presence of the papal nuncio, was giving wrongful legitimation to a fraudulent government. Romero rightly suspected that the seminarians had learned of the UCA's investigation from their Jesuit professors, and regarded their protest as a dangerous foray into politics. As one Jesuit, Father Juan Hernández Pico, recalled, Romero responded to the protest by making "the problem his personal issue. The pope and his nuncio had been attacked, and the hierarchy of the church had been insulted. How could it be worse?"[12]

Romero then "started to actively support the expulsion of the Jesuits from the seminary," saying that they "were the ones that were putting ideas into the seminarians' heads and

Father Ignacio Ellacuría in the Jesuit residence at the University of Central America, San Salvador

9 José María Gondra, SJ, "Discurso de la Universidad Centroamericana José Simeón Cañas en la firma del contrato con el BID," *Planteamiento universitario 1989*, 12.

10 William T. Cavanaugh, "The Ecclesiologies of Medellín and the Lessons of the Base Communities," Cross Currents (Spring 1994): 72.

11 Second Gen. Conference of Latin American Bishops, "Document on Justice," 13.

12 Interview with Juan Hernández Pico, in María López Vigil, *Óscar Romero: Memories in Mosaic* (Washington, DC: Ecumenical Program on Central America and the Caribbean, 2000), 51.

had to go." Romero added ominously, "If they're not removed, we reserve the right to take other measures." This was a threat (at least in part) to bring the matter to the attention of Vatican officials, something Romero actually did on this and other issues. In the end, the Jesuits were removed after fifty years of service and "Monseñor Romero took charge of the seminary." Pico says, "He was satisfied. Orthodoxy had triumphed." Years later Archbishop Romero would apologize to Father Amando López (formerly part of the seminary faculty) for his role in pushing the Jesuits out of the seminary. But in 1972, he was content.

1974–1977 Romero's Personal Conversion: Santiago de María

In 1974, Romero was named bishop of a rural diocese about seventy miles southeast of San Salvador called Santiago de María in Usulután. Here he would remain for the next three years. During this period, something in Romero began to change. His coworkers would later point to Romero's encounter with the terrible suffering of rural farm workers as decisive; these experiences opened his heart and mind to Medellín's preferential option for the poor.[13]

Still, Romero wasn't ready for public confrontations. At one o'clock in the morning on June 21, 1975, members of the National Guard entered Tres Calles, a village in Romero's diocese, ransacking the houses of five farm workers in a search for weapons and murdering the unarmed men in front of their families. Zacarias Diez and Juan Macho, Passionist priests working in the diocese, recall that they and other colleagues told Romero, "We must do something, bishop,"[14] and proposed several forms of public response. "But Monseñor was on another wavelength and didn't think like us." Instead, Romero wrote an anguished letter to his friend President Molina and a summary of

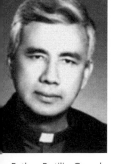

Father Rutilio Grande (July 5, 1928– March 12, 1977)

13 Interview of Bishop Gregorio Rosa Chávez by Robert Lassalle-Klein, San Salvador, November 12, 2009.
14 James R. Brockman, *Romero: A Life* (Maryknoll, NY: Orbis Books, 1989), 61.

the events for the Salvadoran bishops. Looking back, the priests reflect: "It is true; he did something. It was an energetic protest and a strong denouncement." On the other hand, however, "it was not public. It was private, since he still believed that denunciations from authority to authority were more effective."

Later that year, in December 1975, Pope Paul VI published his apostolic exhortation *Evangelii nuntiandi,* linking evangelization in the modern world to prophetic denunciations of poverty and oppression. To many in Latin America, it sounded as if the pope was echoing Medellín's declaration of a preferential option for the poor. According to those close to Romero at the time, Paul VI's words prompted him to reconsider the high priority he had given to maintaining good relations between the church and the government. In the face of state-sponsored violence against his people, and the vilification of his clergy for educating and defending them, Romero gradually came to accept Medellín's discernment that God was calling the Latin American church to support and defend the poor.

Romero's Social Conversion: 1977 The Death of Rutilio Grande

Romero's role in the dismissal of the Jesuits as directors of El Salvador's diocesan seminary in 1972 was only the latest in a series of skirmishes between conservative Salvadoran bishops and the Jesuits. Already in 1970, the bishops had rejected the nomination of the Jesuit priest Rutilio Grande as rector of the seminary in response to the Jesuits' Medellín-inspired agenda there, according to Rodolfo Cardenal, a Jesuit priest. Father Grande reacted to this vote of no confidence by taking a leave of absence from the seminary faculty to study new pastoral approaches in Peru. When he returned in September 1972, around the time of Romero's takeover of the seminary from the Jesuits, his services as a professor were no longer required

Archbishop Óscar Romero (August 15, 1917– March 24, 1980)

and he was assigned as pastor to a parish church in the town of Aguilares. Over the next five years this parish was to become the site of a new Jesuit ministry among rural farm workers, the poorest Salvadorans. Father Grande had traded the comfortable confines of the diocesan seminary for a dangerous new rural ministry among the country's increasingly restive farm workers.

As a result of these and similar initiatives, Father Grande, Ignacio Ellacuría, and other Jesuits were soon accused of being "communists in sheep's clothing" by organizations like the Committee for the Defense of the Fatherland. This explosive rhetoric reaped its predictable harvest on March 12, 1977, when Father Grande was ambushed by the national police, taken from his jeep, and executed.

Less than three weeks before Rutilio Grande's killing, Romero had been appointed as archbishop of San Salvador, to the consternation of those priests who had been most active in advocating for the poor. Both they and the political conservatives who had applauded Romero's appointment were in for a surprise. As Romero later put it, "Father Grande's death and the death of other priests after his impelled me to take an energetic attitude before the government."[15] Despite the archbishop's differences with the Jesuits, he and Grande had been friends. "I remember that because of Father Grande's death I made a statement that I would not attend any official acts until this situation [ascertaining who had killed Rutilio] was clarified." Thus, "a rupture was produced, not by me with the government but [by] the government itself because of its attitude."

Here Romero differentiates his earlier "gradual evolution" toward a personal preferential option for the poor from his decision following Rutilio's death to "respond to the situation in the country as a pastor" by publicly denouncing the government's abuse of human rights. Romero, it seems, underwent two conversions: first a *personal conversion,* characterized by his gradual decision in Santiago de María to assume personal responsibility for the suffering of his people; and second, a *socio-political conversion* following the assassination of Rutilio. After this second conversion, Romero began to publicly address the systematic and ongoing violations of human rights in the country.

Ellacuría, reflecting on this second conversion of his former opponent Romero, would later write that Rutilio Grande's killing confronted the archbishop with three imperatives:[16]

1. A demand to grasp the reality of Father Grande's priestly ministry with the peasant farm workers of Aguilares and why that ministry led to his death;

2. An ethical demand to assume public responsibility as part of his mission as archbishop to accompany and defend the terrorized peasants of Aguilares and El Salvador whom Father Grande left behind; and

3. A praxis-related demand as archbishop to help those peasants, both within the church and in Salvadoran society.

Archbishop Romero, Spiritual Leader of El Salvador

1977–1980

Three months after Father Grande's death, Archbishop Romero drove to the deceased priest's parish of Aguilares. The town had recently been subjected to a full-scale siege by the military in an action appropriately named Operation Rutilio. Soldiers had taken over the town, shot an elderly sacristan as he rang the church bells, arrested and deported the town's three Jesuit priests, and assassinated about fifty people including campesino leaders. In coming to Aguilares, Archbishop Romero's mission was to install a new pastor and celebrate Mass with the terrorized community.

15 Interview of Archbishop Óscar Romero, December 14, 1979, Tommie Sue Montgomery, *Revolution in El Salvador: From Civil Strife to Civil Peace* (Boulder, CO: Westview Press, 1995), 95.

16 Ignacio Ellacuría, "Monseñor Romero, un enviado de Dios para salvar a su pueblo," *Escritos teológicos,* III (UCA Editores, 2002), 93–100; reprinted from *ECA* 19 (1990): 5–10.

The service ended with a procession of the Blessed Sacrament out of the church, Archbishop Romero in the rear and the crowd in front. Jon Sobrino, who was present, offers a remarkable description of what happened next. As the crowd flowed into the square in front of the church, armed troops were stationed in front of the town hall opposite. As the procession approached the soldiers, the crowd stopped, uneasy and afraid. Sobrino writes:

> We had no idea what might happen. . . . [So] we all instinctively turned around and looked at Monseñor Romero, who was bringing up the rear, holding the monstrance. *"¡Adelante!"* (Forward!), said Monseñor Romero. And we went right ahead. The procession ended without incident. From that moment forward, Monseñor Romero was the symbolic leader of El Salvador. He made no such claim. He had sought no such thing. But this is the way it was. From then on Monseñor Romero led us, marching at our head. He had been transformed into the central reference point for the church and for the country. Nothing of any importance occurred in our country over the next three years without our all turning to Monseñor Romero for guidance and direction, for leadership.[17]

Over those three years, Romero served as spiritual leader and shepherd for the nation, speaking to his fellow Salvadorans in weekly radio sermons that drew huge audiences. In one such sermon on March 23, 1980, Romero called on Salvadoran soldiers to refuse to obey orders that violated God's law. The next day he was shot and killed while saying Mass. The sniper had been hired by former Major Robert D'Aubuisson, a leader in El Salvador's right-wing faction.[18]

1980–1989 ## Learning from a Martyr

Ellacuría responded to the archbishop's death by writing an homage whose title alone shows

how much had changed in the eight years since Romero had evicted the Jesuits from the seminary: "Monseñor Romero, a Man Sent by God to Save His Country." Romero, wrote Ellacuría, "was the teacher" and the UCA "was the assistant," Romero "was the voice and . . . [the UCA] was the echo."

In the same article, Ellacuría describes the lessons that the UCA learned from its mentor.[19] The Jesuits learned how "to historicize the power of the gospel" by running the university, like the archdiocese, with special concern for the needs of the poor. Previously the university had focused almost exclusively on El Salvador's elites. But Archbishop Romero showed the UCA that when the church embraced the sufferings and hopes of El Salvador's poor majorities, "what had been an opaque, amorphous, and ineffective word became a torrent of life to which the people drew near in order to quench their thirst." Romero's example demonstrated how "the power of the gospel could become a transformative historical force."

Accordingly, after the archbishop's death the UCA became a new kind of Christian university – one focused on making God's love of the poor real in El Salvador. For example, it sought ways to increase participation by the country's dispossessed majorities in the debate over how to resolve the country's civil war. Ellacuría summarized his vision in a 1982 address at Santa Clara University, arguing that "a university of Christian inspiration is one that focuses all its university activity . . . within the illuminating horizon of . . . a Christian preferential option for the poor."[20] The university's task, he said, is to serve as an "intellectual support for those who . . . possess truth and reason . . . but who do not have the academic arguments to justify and legitimate them."

It was for courageously living out this

17 Doggett, *Death Foretold*, 27.
18 United Nations, *Report on the Commission on the Truth for El Salvador*, 127.

19 All quotes from Ellacuría in this section are from Ellacuría, "Monseñor Romero, un enviado de Dios para salvar a su pueblo," 93–100.
20 Ignacio Ellacuría, "Discurso de graduación en la Universidad de Santa Clara," *Escritos universitarios* (San Salvador: UCA Editores, 1999), 226.

Gervasio Sánchez

vocation that Father Ellacuría and his brother Jesuits gave up their lives.

Blood and Ink

When the murdered priests were found on the morning of November 16, 1989, a blood-soaked copy of Jürgen Moltmann's book *The Crucified God* was discovered near the body of Father Moreno. Today it is preserved in the university's museum, just feet from where its owner died. It serves as a visceral sign of the cost of this ultimately unsuccessful attempt to silence the voice of scholars who, for almost two decades, had documented the sufferings of the people of El Salvador. The blood and ink mingled on its pages serve as a fitting symbol of the faith, hope, and love that animated these men.

In 2009, Jon Sobrino wrote a letter to his deceased friend Ellacuría titled "Monseñor Romero and You":

> People know that both of you were eloquent prophets and martyrs, . . . [but] I like to remember another important similarity, which is how you began. Each of you was given a Christian and Salvadoran torch, and without any kind of discernment made the fundamental choice to keep it burning. Monseñor Romero received it from Rutilio Grande the night they killed him. And when Monseñor Romero died, you picked it up."[21]

21 Jon Sobrino, "Monseñor Romero y tú," Carta a Ellacuría 2009, *www.foroellacuria. org/otra_mirada.htm*.

Sobrino believes it is crucial to remember "that in El Salvador there was a grand tradition" which was "passed from hand to hand" of "dedication and love for the poor, confrontation with oppressors, steadiness in conflict, and the hope and the dream [of the kingdom of God]" grounded in "the Jesus of the gospel and the mystery of his God." And he insists, "We must not squander that legacy and we need to make it available to the young."

Twenty-five years after the martyrdom of the UCA Jesuits and thirty-five years after the martyrdom of Archbishop Romero, what can we learn from their example? In 1982, Ellacuría counseled graduating seniors to respond by following the example of the company of martyrs who preceded them:

> Just place your whole human heart before the reality of a crucified world, and ask yourselves the three questions that Ignatius of Loyola put to himself as he stood before [an image of the crucified Christ], the representative of all those who are crucified: What have I done for this world? What am I doing for it now? And above all, what should I do? The answers lie both in your personal and academic responsibility.[22]

22 Ellacuria, "Discurso de graduación," 228.

Ignacio Ellacuría speaking at an ecumenical service in San Salvador, March 1989, eight months before his death

Dispatch from Ferguson

Obtaining Justice for a Wounded Community

A former gang member who graduated from Harvard, Eugene F. Rivers III is pastor of the Azusa Christian Community in Dorchester, Massachusetts. His programs to get churches involved in curbing youth violence in his inner-city Boston neighborhood have been emulated nationwide. We asked him for his insights on the unrest in Ferguson, Missouri, prompted by the killing of Michael Brown, an unarmed eighteen-year-old, by a police officer.

Young people are still protesting in Ferguson almost three months after the death of Michael Brown on August 9, 2014. Their perseverance is impressive; they press on after the national media have left and after people have stopped flocking to St. Louis to support them. But how likely is it that they will accomplish the goals of their protest, even after all their efforts?

The community's solidarity and determination in its response to the shooting reveals two things. First, it confirms that the ability of social media to galvanize revolutions is not limited to distant places like Iran. Second, these young people and the adults who support them were just discovering the power they potentially had at their fingertips. When Michael Brown, an eighteen-year-old black man, was shot down in the middle of the day by a white police officer, Torrey Russell, another young black man, announced on social media that he was going to the police station to demand some answers. He was astonished to find himself heading a large crowd of youth. The next day, Rev. Traci Blackmon, a United Church of Christ minister, took to social media to declare her intention of joining the young people's protest. She too was greeted by an unexpected crowd of supporters at the police station. Kareem Jackson, a St. Louis rapper, stepped up when women and children were assaulted with tear gas canisters and defended them by tossing back the canisters. This young man talked down gang leaders and other youth who were ready to arm themselves and take on the police who publicly referred to black people as "coon" and "nigguh."

Though social media brought the protesters together, it is the underlying problems in the community that have fueled their staying power. Ferguson is Birmingham, Alabama, circa 1963. Only three officers out of a police force of

An impromptu memorial to Michael Brown

Photograph by Loavesofbread

aste of Honey
HAIR SALON

CHILDREN'S CITY
DISCOUNT CLOTHING
314-524-2254

Photograph by Scott Olson / Getty Images

fifty-three are black, though 67 percent of Ferguson's residents are. Fines and court fees for traffic violations and other infractions of the law were the second largest source of income for the city in 2013. This creates an incentive for police to ticket drivers for every offense, no matter how minor, and this practice is highly racialized: 93 percent of arrests, 86 percent of traffic stops, and 92 percent of vehicle searches in Ferguson involved blacks, even though a smaller fraction of blacks stopped were carrying illegal substances compared to whites. There are very few black elected officials, due in part to blacks' withdrawal from the electoral system. Roughly 30 percent of blacks in St. Louis City and St. Louis County, where Ferguson is located, live below the poverty level, compared to a poverty rate of 8 percent among whites.

This highly unjust, racially unequal system has transformed a protest about the death of one young man. It has become more than a quest for justice for him; it becomes a demand for access to a better life for all the young people like him who suffer under an inequitable system. But will they get justice for either Michael Brown or themselves?

Here are two important obstacles to obtaining justice in Ferguson: the laws of the land and the trauma endured by the black community. First, laws governing the conduct of police officers who use lethal force have an extremely high bar of proof. It must be demonstrated that the officer intentionally used more force in the situation than was necessary. Therefore it is unlikely, though not impossible, that Officer Darren Wilson will be convicted.

The second factor, how the incident traumatized the community, affects the likelihood of justice for the young people and children who still live in Ferguson. Michael Brown's body lay in the street for over four hours. His mother screamed and pleaded to be allowed to go to him, but she was denied. His stepfather asked to be permitted to cover his body with a sheet but was not allowed by the police officers. A mother taking her daughter home unexpectedly encountered the scene as Michael Brown's blood soaked into the asphalt. Residents crowded around in distress.

In response to the protests demanding justice the police barricaded four square blocks,

Plywood covered storefronts near the Ferguson police station in November, 2014. Businesses were bracing for possible vandalism if a grand jury declined to press charges against Darren Wilson, the officer who killed Michael Brown.

Photographs by Jamelle Bouie / Wikimedia

Left,
a police
sharpshooter
in position
at a protest
in Ferguson,
Missouri

Right,
protestors
gather at the
police station

preventing children from going to school and residents from going to work for several days. Just recounting his concern for other young men like him brought one man to tears. This traumatized community is ill-equipped to handle conflagrations that will likely erupt again if Officer Wilson is not brought to justice. What is more, though the community is keenly aware of the underlying systemic injustices they face, the anger and frustration aroused by the recent events may get in the way of their obtaining justice. The leaders of the protest are less focused on the tough questions of how to address the intractable structural issues they face than they are on continuing to protest.

The situation is compounded by a failure of leadership in the black churches in the area. Granted, the local black Pentecostal clergy were impressive, feeding poor families when most of the stores shut down due to the rioting, and cleaning up the neighborhood at 7 a.m. after each night of rioting. Nonetheless a substantial gap exists between the youth leading the protests and prominent church leaders, both local and national. In fact, recently the youth explicitly expressed their disappointment in the lack of a plan of action proffered by national figures who spoke at a march organized by local clergy.

What is needed in Ferguson is a sustainable strategy for the long game, with measurable outcomes: reducing violence among youth and increasing employment and education. Those who work within mainstream institutions, such as businessmen, politicians, university faculty, and philanthropists, must, in the short term, provide

jobs for some of these youth. Many continue to protest in part because they cannot find employment into which to channel their energy. Then, over the next year or two, programs that address the most urgent needs – employment, training, and education – must be designed and implemented. A strategic plan to integrate the police force in Ferguson must be put in place to address the alienation experienced by youth and other community members. A major voter-registration drive and get-out-the-vote effort is also essential to ensure representation of the community in local government. And a plan is needed to reduce the reliance of Ferguson and other suburbs of St. Louis on fines for their fiscal health.

These inside players must also collaborate with clergy and activists. Black ministers, for their part, must put in place programs to foster healing among traumatized youth and other residents. Only as the powerful emotions aroused by the situation are de-escalated can the community fully participate in long-term planning. Ministers must build relationships with young men and women, meeting them on their own terms. Street patrols led by clergy are one effective strategy to begin connecting with youth. From this base, young people can be referred to programs in which clergy can mentor them.

While the verdict of the justice system in the case of Officer Wilson is beyond the control of the community, there is a role for all to play in obtaining justice in Ferguson by beginning to dismantle the system of racial inequity that traps youth like Michael Brown. ➤

Soldier of the Lamb

WHAT I LEARNED FROM LARRY

JASON LANDSEL

Photographs provided by author

The prophet Isaiah appeared in our previous issue, hammering a red-hot sword into plowshares in the "Forerunners" column by artist Jason Landsel, which features men and women of God through the ages. The model for this striking portrait of Isaiah was Larry Mason, a friend of Jason's who is a Vietnam veteran, graduate of the streets of New York City, and brother in the Bruderhof community.

When Larry was diagnosed with aggressive cancer in September, Jason was working on artwork for this page. He set the project aside to care for Larry, who had adopted Jason's family as his own. In place of a painting, Jason sent us this reflection in honor of his friend, who died on October 23.

At the age of twenty-four, Larry was drafted into the United States Army in 1967. He was looking for purpose. Having spent most of his childhood on the streets and in and out of state institutions, he had married young and had two daughters before the relationship fell apart. Now the army took six years of Larry's life, including three years in Vietnam where Larry saw combat. Some memories he shared with us; most of them not. He later would say: "I killed, and I saw people killed. I got caught up in the war spirit, and kept re-enlisting until in 1974 they told me, 'You've had enough, go home.' But I had no real home; normal society had nothing to offer me anymore."

The military gave him an honorable discharge but declared him "mentally unfit for assimilation." Larry didn't disagree with this assessment. He returned to the streets, dealing drugs and living for a while in an improvised army-style camp on Staten Island with other homeless veterans. In 1977 he was convicted of robbery and attempted murder, serving four years of a ten year sentence in a range of New York State prisons including Attica.

Paroled in 1981, it didn't take long before he resumed his old life. He later recalled:

> I knew it was only a matter of time before I was dead. I felt like blowing my head off, but I knew that a true soldier dies with his boots on and never by his own hand. One day I went in desperation to my parole officer and told him to lock me up again. To give him a reason, I laid the pistol I was carrying on his desk. Instead of sending me back to jail, he directed me to the Bowery Mission in Manhattan, a Bible-based program to help people find purpose in life and a new chance. Though he wasn't a Christian, he told me, "Maybe here you will find what you are looking for." He gave me some money for the taxi ride; I used it for a bottle of wine, and walked. On the way I stopped at a small church where, sitting in the chapel, I was suddenly overcome with despair and wept tears of pain for the first time since I was a child. Something happened to me in that church. I ended up staying several years at the Bowery Mission.

After seven years at the Bowery Mission, Larry joined the Bruderhof community in upstate New

Larry Mason, a formerly homeless Vietnam veteran, taking a break with young friends while cleaning up an abandoned chapel

Will we follow the Jesus who sleeps on heating grates?

York. He was a hard worker in the community's factory, making equipment for people with disabilities. Active in the life of the church, he often assisted ministers at baptisms and weddings. He was known for his free-spirited renditions of "Amazing Grace" and for occasionally showing up in war paint and a kilt. Off-hours, he dedicated much of his time to mentoring children and young people.

One of his efforts was the "Lake of Fire Rescue Team" – a yearlong project to renovate an abandoned chapel in the woods (it had belonged to a long-discontinued Catholic summer camp). The members of the Rescue Team, apart from Larry, were a group of middle-school-age boys. In cooperation with their parents, Larry gave the young men lessons in work ethic, survival skills, and – most importantly to him – Bible study.

"Stay in the Word," was one of Larry's repeated messages to young people. They listened because it was obvious how acutely he felt his own need for God every minute and every day. He suffered from PTSD and was tormented by nightmares of Vietnam, prison, and the streets. Maybe that's why he especially loved Paul's exhortation to "put on the armor of God" in Ephesians 6: "Our fight is not with

people; it is against the leaders and the powers and the spirits of darkness in this world." With a hand on his well-worn Bible, Larry would quote Psalm 119, "I have hidden your word in my heart that I might not sin against you."

When we buried Larry, one of his close friends read the words of Isaiah 53:

> He was despised and rejected by others;
> a man of suffering and acquainted
>   with infirmity;
> and as one from whom others hide their faces
> he was despised, and we held him
>   of no account.

This was the Jesus that Larry knew. And where does his story leave us? Will we answer the same call from the Jesus that Larry followed – the Jesus that walks the battle fields, the Jesus who sleeps on heating grates or in subway stations? Will we embrace and recognize the Christ in all who seek him? Or will we – as the prophet Isaiah so aptly describes – be put off by foul mannerisms or appearance?

I pray for thousands more Larrys to join with our community. May we be found ready.

Jason Landsel, a contributing artist to this magazine, lives in the Woodcrest community in upstate New York.